Serve and Obey

Serve and Obey

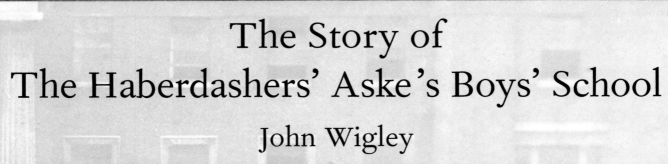

The Story of
The Haberdashers' Aske's Boys' School

John Wigley

JAMES X JAMES

© The Haberdashers' Aske's Boys' School, 2007

ISBN 978 1 903942 80 2

First published in 2007
by James & James (Publishers) Ltd
a member of Third Millennium Information
2-5 Benjamin Street
London
EC1M 5QL

www.tmiltd.com

Project Editor and image research: Susan Millership
Design: Vimbai Shire
Production: Bonnie Murray

Photography: John Spragg and Roy Wooding, ICS

Printed and bound by
Butler & Tanner
Frome
United Kingdom

Picture Acknowledgements

Many of the illustrations come from material in the School Archive and individual Old Scholars' collections and the publishers are grateful for permission to reproduce pictures from the following: Mary Evans Library 10, 28; Metropolitan archives 14–15, 16, 21, 24; National Portrait Gallery, London 10, 16, Jonathan Ratter 89 (bottom right and middle), 97, 98 (bottom middle and right), 99 (top), 100 (all), 101, 103 (bottom), 104 (all), 105; the agency (london) ltd 137; The Hampstead Museum/Burgh House 64-65.

Illustrations

JACKET, FRONT: View of Aldenham House.
BACK: Coat of Arms.
HALF TITLE: Coat of Arms.
TITLE PAGE: The Hoxton School, 1876. Statue of Robert Aske in foreground.

Contents

Acknowledgements

This illustrated history is intended to make Haberdashers' past accessible to all members of the school community, not only boys and old boys, but teachers and parents, and prospective pupils and their parents.

I am grateful to Margaret Taylor, Pat McGowan and Sheila Wiltshire, and to the former pupils and teachers who also gave tape-recorded interviews; Lord Brittan, Keith Cheney, Basil Flashman, George Garnett, Lawrence Goldman, and John Lear.

I am indebted to former teachers and pupils who sent me their reminiscences, although some of the Old Haberdashers (OHs) have since sadly died. I have acknowledged such accounts in the text. I owe a particular debt to John Carleton, David and Flora Griffiths, Leo Guidon, David Jones, Dennis L. Cooper-Jones, John Holmes, David Lidington MP, Ashley Blaker and Brian Sewell.

The staffs of the British Library, the Metropolitan Archives, and the National Archives were invariably efficient and helpful when providing the printed and manuscript material on which the book is largely based, notably the records of the Haberdashers' Company preserved in the Guildhall Library.

I have also used several secondary sources: M.I. Batten, The Architecture of Dr Robert Hooke FRS (Walpole Society, London, 25, 1936–37), J.R. Meredith, The Foundation and Early History of Aske's Hospital at Hoxton, 1689-1755 (1964), J.R. Avery, The Story of Aldenham House (1961), Andrew Lawrence, The Aldenham House Gardens (1988), Ian W. Archer, The History of the Haberdashers' Company (1991) and Hamish Adam, Confessions of a Boarder (2002).

I was well supported by Keith Cheney (the School Archivist), Stephen Wilson (who conducted the interviews), and Jon Corrall (the Senior Master, who suggested that I undertake the work). Jon and Stephen kindly read successive drafts. Peter Spence (the School's Director of External Relations) coordinated the project.

Hamish MacGibbon, Susan Millership and Robert Harries of James & James gave expert advice on the structure and style of the text.

I thank them all.

John Wigley
MAY 2007

Foreword

John Wigley's admirable history of Haberdashers' shows that Habs, as it is usually called by the boys, has had a distinguished history and a remarkable rise to fame, and its pages and illustrations catch the atmosphere and flavour of this very special place.

This book reflects our core aims as stated in the Prospectus: 'To challenge bright boys to achieve the highest standards, to develop a sense of community and shared values, and to support parents in preparing their sons for a fulfilled life.'

Its later pages give a snapshot of life here today; of the challenges and the opportunities in this most academic, multi-cultural and vibrant of schools. In academic study and in extra-curricular activities of all kinds we prepare our pupils for the best of universities, the best of careers and the best of adult lives.

The 2005 inspection resulted in a glowing testimonial, confirming our position as one of the country's leading independent schools. Outstanding amongst our obvious strengths was the quality of our pupils. They were described as 'exceptionally well-motivated learners', 'making rapid progress and attaining high examination results', whilst participating in a flourishing programme of over 70 different activities.

In acknowledging our excellence, the inspectors gave particular praise to the quality of our pupils' personal development. Pastoral care was rated as exceptionally good, resulting in a school where all pupils are valued and racial harmony is of the highest quality. The overall tone is of 'an outstandingly well-integrated school community' supported by dedicated and hard-working staff.

The Preparatory School shared the limelight. According to the inspectors, the Prep.'s 'excellent academic record' and 'care for each individual' contribute to 'an excellent ethos in which a positive joy in learning can flourish from an early age.' In November 2006 The Sunday Times judged it 'Preparatory School of the Year'.

We are now entering a new and exciting phase. The Governors have recently established the innovative Haberdashers' Foundation. We are pushing forward with a programme of improvement to our buildings and facilities, and are pursuing a course of development for our staff, to attract and retain the best teachers — our most important resource. We have expanded the Prep.'s intake with classes of 5+ and 6+ boys, and in 2006 decided to open a Pre-Prep. School in nearby Park Street.

All this will ensure that Haberdashers' continues to flourish in the years to come.

Peter Hamilton
MAY 2007

1

The School's Origins

B y the mid-14th century London's haberdashers were dealers in small drapery and associated wares, such as beads, buttons, laces, ribbons and tape, needles and thread, and were credited with importing the first pins into England. In 1371 a set of ordinances was drawn up for the Haberdashers as a distinct fraternity with their patron saint, St Katherine of Alexandria, and they were well enough known for Chaucer to refer to them in his *Prologue to The Canterbury Tales.*

In 1446 the Haberdashers' fraternity was granted armorial bearings, and on 3 June 1448 it received a charter from King Henry VI (1421–71), incorporating it as the 'Guild of St Katherine the Virgin of Haberdashers in the City of London'. In 1458 the guild's status was confirmed when it acquired the site of a hall, and in 1538 it was recognised as eighth in the hierarchy of the great 12 livery companies.

In 1588 a future Master of the Company, Martin Bond, commanded the soldiers which Queen Elizabeth I (1558–1603) reviewed at Tilbury as the Armada sailed up the Channel. (By coincidence, a young poet, James Aske, made the only contemporary record of her famous speech.) Some members of the Company were Puritans and in 1683 Henry Cornish, in 1680 its Master, was executed for his part in the Rye House Plot, an attempt to assassinate King Charles II (1660–85) and his brother James. Within two weeks of succeeding to the throne James II (1685–88) gave the company a revised Charter naming Robert Aske as the new Master. He was elected on 5 March after taking the oath contained in the 1661 Corporation Act, 'That it is not lawful upon any pretence whatever to take arms against the king.'

Robert Aske, 1619–89. From a portrait in the Headmaster's study.

Aske's executors: (TOP) Dr John Tillotson, Dean of Canterbury, 1672–91, and then Archbishop; (ABOVE) Dr John Sharp, Dean of Norwich, 1681–89, later Archbishop of York.

Robert Aske was probably descended from Richard Aske, a younger son of the Aske family of Richmond in the North Riding of Yorkshire. The fortified tower built by the Askes in the Middle Ages can still be seen at Aske Hall, now the home of the Marquess of Zetland. In the 14th century Richard de Aske married the heiress to an estate at Aughton in the East Riding, and Aughton Church contains monuments to him and his wife. One of his great-grandsons, Christopher, built the tower of Aughton Church, which bears his coat of arms and Latin inscription, and in 1536 another great- grandson, Robert, a Gray's Inn lawyer, led the Pilgrimage of Grace, in fact a rebellion against King Henry VIII (1509–48), and was executed in York on 12 July 1537.

During the later 16th century the Askes married into the Fairfax family, and Sir Thomas Fairfax, Commander in Chief of the Parliamentary Army in the Civil War, secured John Aske the job of helping Oliver Cromwell's Solicitor General, John Cooke, to draw up the charge against King Charles I in 1649 and to assist at the trial which led to his execution. As a regicide, John Aske went in fear of his life: in 1650 a royalist assassin killed the wrong man, the ambassador to Spain, Anthony Ascham.

Robert Aske was born on 24 February 1619, son of Robert and Margery Aske. His father was a well-connected draper from the parish of St Mary Woolchurch; his stepfather, John Passmore, a wealthy armourer of St Michael's Cornhill, who in May 1634 apprenticed him to John Trott, a Haberdasher and East India Company merchant. Aske flourished, becoming a merchant in raw silk, dealing in property in London and Leicestershire, and underwriting insurance. In 1643 he became a Freeman of the Company, and in 1666 a member of its Court of Assistants. On 17 February 1679 he married Mary Bonfoy, widow of Nicholas Bonfoy, an Alderman and brother of Sir Thomas Bonfoy, a member of the Clothworkers' Company. Aske's marriage licence described him as a widower, but there is no known record of a previous marriage, and no evidence of any children.

As a member of a landed family, Robert Aske had a coat of arms ('Or, three bars azure') and a crest ('An old man's head, front face, couped at the shoulder proper'), but his strongest links were with the City of London, where he had family ties with the Drapers' and Goldsmiths' Companies. By the 1660s he was a wealthy man. In 1666 he was nominated as Sheriff of the City of London and paid a fine of £620 for refusing to serve. In 1668 he was elected Master of the Haberdashers' Company and was again fined for refusing to serve. However, during the next decade he took an active part in raising money to rebuild his parish church and the Company's hall, both of which had been destroyed by the Great Fire of 1666, as had his own house.

Aske's time as Master of the Company came to an abrupt end when in September 1687 King James II appointed a new Master. Aske was therefore living in obscurity when in May 1688 James ordered his Second Declaration of Indulgence, giving Catholics freedom of worship, to be read from the pulpit in all Anglican churches. The Archbishop of Canterbury and six other bishops refused to read it. James flew into a rage: 'This is a surprise to me. I did not expect this from you. This is a standard of rebellion.' The Archbishop and bishops were advised by the Dean of Canterbury, Dr John Tillotson. Aske had named him and the Dean of Norwich, Dr John Sharp, as his executors. He had known them both whilst they were clergymen in London.

Aske's will followed the precedent set by several earlier usually childless and actually Puritan members of the Company. In 1594 Thomas Aldersey had bequeathed money for a school at Bunbury in Cheshire, in 1615 William Jones had endowed one at Monmouth, in 1656 William Adams had left funds for one at Newport in Shropshire, and in 1666 Throckmorton Trotman's will provided for one at Bunhill Fields in London. Aske almost certainly knew Adams and Trotman, for they were his contemporaries in the Company, and as Master for some two years he would have realised that the Company was punctilious in handling such bequests.

Robert Aske made his will on 18 January 1689. He bequeathed £20,000 and the residue of his estate in trust to the Haberdashers' Company to buy a piece of land within one mile or thereabouts of London, to build on it an almshouse for 20 poor single freemen of the company, to purchase enough land to yield an income of £20 a year for each of them; and to use any remainder 'to be layd out in Lands for the maintenance of soe many poore Boyes … at 20 pounds each for Meat drinke cloathing and Schooling.' Two days later he added a codicil appointing the Company's Master, four Wardens and Assistants as governors of 'the said Hospital', provided that the 'twenty poore Boyes shall be ffreemens Sonnes', and stipulated 'if it happen that hereafter that any of the Revenue shall fall short, the same shall be deducted out of the Revenue for the poore Boyes'. Aske died on 27 January and on 1 February was buried in the church of St Mary Aldermanbury.

Aske's executors proved the will on 4 February. It was read at the Company's Court of Assistants on 6 February. On 8 March the Court set up a Committee to manage the bequest and on 13 March Tillotson and Sharp passed Aske's assets, stock and debts to the Company, to be realised for the Hospital. By the end of 1690 it had received the £20,000 stipulated in the will plus a residue of £11,905 1s. 0d., a very large sum indeed by the values of that time.

The Committee approached Dr Robert Hooke. Like Sir Christopher Wren, he was a celebrated architect and scientist and a Fellow of the Royal Society. Wren had designed Chelsea Hospital, a home for old soldiers, and Hooke Bethlehem Hospital (colloquially called Bedlam), a lunatic asylum. They collaborated to design the Monument, the City's memorial to the Great Fire, still the world's tallest free-standing stone column. Thus Hooke seemed a sound source of advice.

On 18 March 1689 the Committee invited Hooke, Tillotson and Sharp to dinner in Romer's coffee house, where Hooke agreed to design the Hospital. The Committee visited and considered various sites on the northern outskirts of London, in May 1690 accepted Hooke's advice to buy land in Hoxton, and in June purchased some 20 acres for £2,000. Hooke had already produced a design, and by December followed it up with a plan and a model, as the Court prepared to draw up a contract, to lay the foundation stone and to start to build.

Before it did so, the Company secured an Act of Parliament vesting corporate control and governance of the Hospital in the Master and Wardens of the Haberdashers' Company and their successors. On 20 December 1690 King William III and Queen Mary II gave their Royal Assent to 'An Act for the Settling a Charity given by Robert Aske Esq., to the Company of Haberdashers of London'. In part, the Act read:

The Monument, designed by Robert Hooke and Christopher Wren to commemorate the Great Fire of London, 1666.

That for ever hereafter there shall be in the Town of Hoxton in the Parish of St Leonard Shoreditch, One Hospital of twenty poor Single Decayed freemen of the said Company of Haberdashers, and the Maintenance of twenty poor Decayed freemens Sons with Meat, Drink, Clothing and Schooling; Which shall be called, The Hospital at Hoxton, of the Foundation of Robert Aske Esquire.

That the said Governours shall Nominate and Appoint, with the Approbation and License of the Lord Bishop of London, some Learned and Discreet Schoolmaster to read Prayers and Preach, and Teach the Scholars in such Learning and good Manners as they the said Governours in their Discretion shall Appoint and Direct.

In other words, the Act established a 'Hospital' consisting of an almshouse for 20 resident old men and a school for 20 boy boarders. Its head was to be an Anglican clergyman who would be chaplain to the old men and master to the boys.

Building the Hospital caused problems. The leading craftsman objected to the Company's contract. It dismissed the original workers, accused the bricklayers and the carpenters of overcharging, and the two principal carpenters sued for non-payment in the Court of King's Bench. During 1694 it abandoned Hooke's plan for a central cupola. Tillotson's biographer Birch recorded that Hooke attributed the high building costs to additions and alterations to the first design and to his failure to hire and contract with the workmen personally. Building was unfinished in the autumn of 1695 when the first 20 'poor Single Decayed freemen' moved in.

The Hospital was a magnificent building, some 340 feet from north to south, with its principal front to the east. A central pedimented block had lower ranges to its north and south, and each ended in a higher wing, which was linked to the centre block by an open colonnade on the ground floor of the east front. Surviving engravings show that the design was derived from that of Hooke's Bethlehem Hospital and from the south front of Wren's Chelsea Hospital.

The pediment enclosed a clock, immediately below which was a life-size statue of Aske clothed with a gown and holding a roll of parchment. Inscriptions in Latin and English recorded his munificence. Below the statue was the main door. To the west was a garden and to the southwest a small burial ground. In front of the Hospital was a court surrounded by lime trees, given by a member of the Company in 1695. An entrance gate whose two pillars were each surmounted by a statue representing 'Aske's Hospital Men' led into Pitfield Street, then little more than a country lane.

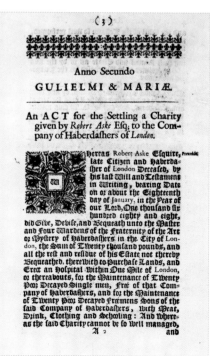

At the centre of the Hospital's ground floor a large hallway led through the building from east to west. To its immediate north was a two-storeyed chapel, to the north of that a staircase (with an entrance to the colonnade), to its north ten sets of rooms for the old men (each set with a lobby, staircase and three chambers), and to their north a further staircase and the north wing (which may in part have contained a library). To the south of the central hallway was a symmetrical pattern: great hall, staircase, ten sets of rooms, the staircase and the south wing (which may have housed the Chaplain and contained the Company's court room). Rooms above the chapel and great hall may have accommodated the school room, the boys' wards (dormitories), matron and maids, and (at a later date) the schoolmaster. The domestic quarters and kitchens were probably in a basement under the central block.

In September 1695 the Company furnished the Hospital, and thereafter took regular inventories. The chapel was given a communion table and linen, two pewter chalices, a communion flagon and plate, a silver communion cup, and a Bible and Book of Common Prayer. The great hall was provided with a handbell for summoning the old men and boys to meals, furnished with two long and two small tables, ten forms, five chairs, two stools, and decorated with 'The picture of Esq. Ask.' The school room was simply equipped with a desk for the master and two desks and forms for the boys. Prominent in the library were three copies of John Foxe's *Book of Martyrs*, first published in 1563, which described and illustrated the persecution of Protestants during the reign of Queen Mary I (1553–58).

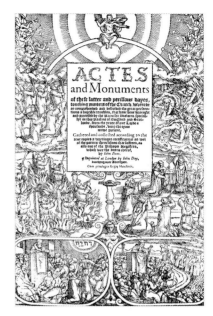

Title page from John Foxe's *Book of Martyrs*.

East front of Aske's Hospital, 1690s.

2

The Early Years

1695–1813

On 5 July 1695 the Company approved 'Statutes and Lawes' for the Hospital. As Governors, the Master and Wardens were to visit the Hospital once a month to inspect its management, the 'pensioners' and the officers, and to report any problems to the Court of Assistants. Audit Day was to be celebrated by dinner on the premises.

The Statutes provided for four officers; a Chaplain to read prayers and preach, a Manciple as steward, a Matron as housekeeper, and a Cook. In September 1695 the Court appointed the first Chaplain, the Revd Thomas Wright MA. He had previously been Schoolmaster at Monmouth and was presently Schoolmaster at Bunhill. The first 20 'pensioners' were admitted to the Hospital during October and November 1695, and on Sunday 24 November its formal opening was marked by the consecration of the chapel and burial ground by Dr Henry Compton, the Bishop of London, one of the brave men who had invited William of Orange to depose James II. The Company provided a gallon of wine for Holy Communion, and the Governors attended in their gowns, hearing one sermon before and one after dinner, which they claimed was conducted with 'gravity and sobriety'.

From June to September 1697 the Court fitted out 'the Long Room' for the boys and in November admitted the first 20. On 20 January 1702 the Court therefore promulgated a second set of Statutes. Revised in 1746, they were in force for over a century, and were framed and read publicly on each anniversary of Aske's birthday.

The boys were to be governed by a Committee of 11 members of the Court of Assistants, including the Master and four Wardens. It was to

ABOVE: Dr Henry Compton, Bishop of London,
1675–1713.

BELOW RIGHT: St Leonard's Church, Shoreditch,
1694.

hear petitions for admission and pass them to the Court, which was to admit only
Freemen's sons and to give preference to those of the Company's officials. Boys had to be
between the ages of nine and 12 and be able to 'read readily', but were not to be admitted
if they were ill, or had a brother in residence. They were all to leave at the age of 15.

The Committee would only admit a boy of proven poverty whose parents or parish of
origin would guarantee to take him back at 15 or when he was expelled, for misbehaviour
including lying, stealing, swearing, or being absent without leave. If a boy inherited £100
or more he would be dismissed and if he became ill he would be removed to an infirmary.
Whilst in the Hospital he would wear a 'gowne and Capp'.

The Schoolmaster was to teach the 'Rudiments of Grammar', to give 'such moderate
Correction as shall be agreeable to prudence', to report on the boys' aptitude, and to
ensure that they went to prayers. In the winter he was to teach from 8 to 11 a.m. and from
1 to 4 p.m., and in the summer from 7 to 11 a.m. and from 1 to 5 p.m. A Writing Master
was to be hired to teach the boys 'to write fair and all manner of needful Arithmetick' on
Tuesday, Thursday and Saturday afternoons.

When the first boys were admitted the Revd John Pridie was appointed Chaplain and
Schoolmaster and paid £40 a year plus free board and lodging. His duties were 'To preach
once every Lord's Day, to read prayers twice every day in the week. To teach the children
English and to Catechise them and to learn them the Rudiments of Grammar.' In June
1698 the Court appointed Mr Serjeant as Writing Master, to teach writing and arithmetic

for £17 a year. In 1705 the Committee
ordered him to attend on Audit Day with
the boys' 'coppy books and Cyfring books'
ready for inspection.

However, in September 1700 Pridie and
all the officers and servants except Mr
Serjeant and the Matron, Mrs Pelcombe,
were dismissed. Henceforth she, rather
than the Chaplain, was to supervise the
maidservants. She also took over the
Manciple's duties and died in office in
1722. In the 1730s one of her successors,
Mrs Frances Smith, pawned the
Communion plate, so in future the
Chaplain prudently kept 'The Book of
Accounts for the Hospitall' in his own
quarters.

In November 1700 the Revd Charles
Lovell MA was elected Chaplain. He
survived doubts about his suitability when
he married, and rebutted complaints from
pensioners that he withheld collection
money due to them from members of the

public attending Holy Communion in the chapel, and that he fed private boarders from the Hospital kitchen. He died in office in January 1713. The Court then appointed the Revd Henry Vaughan who resigned in 1724.

The Hospital's income proved too low to maintain the men and the boys. Most of the £31,905 1s. 0d. the Company had received from Aske's estate by March 1690 had been quickly spent. After buying the land at Hoxton for £2,000, settling debts, legacies and fees of £3,933 5s. 6d., building and furnishing the Hospital cost £11,787 6s. 7d., and buying the estate in Kent claimed £13,211 6s. 0d. Thus £933 2s. 11d. was unaccounted for and there was barely enough ready money to run the Hospital, let alone to meet emergencies such as the great storm of 1703, which stripped its roof of tiles, whose price rose from 21/- to 120/- a thousand.

The Hoxton estate surrounding the Hospital yielded rent of about £80 a year, but the Kent estate proved problematic. Between 1690 and 1694 the Company had bought approximately 1,600 acres of freehold and 450 acres of leasehold land near Ashford. The Company expected rent of some £800 a year and that it would be the main source of the Hospital's income. However, the bills for taxes and repairs proved higher than expected, and after 1708 when the Steward was allowed to submit only net receipts revenue fell rapidly, in 1722 reaching a low point of £287 13s. 0d., despite several inspections by the Master and Wardens.

In May 1708 the Court acted on the terms of the codicil to Aske's will and decided that no more boys would be admitted until there were ten vacancies, and in March 1712 that no vacancies would be filled. By March 1713 only eight boys remained, so Mr Serjeant and their maid were dismissed, and Vaughan given an extra £15 to teach the boys writing and arithmetic, but the school was empty between 1714 and 1739.

Thus from 1714 to 1724 Vaughan had no teaching duties. Nor did his successor, the Revd Arthur Bedford MA, late scholar of Brasenose College, Oxford, a well-known author, controversialist and preacher. In 1705 he had begun a campaign against the theatre, which he claimed promoted blasphemy and idolatry; and in 1706 had started another, to restore psalm singing in church, which he was convinced had originated in Solomon's Temple. He attacked Sir Isaac Newton's *The Chronology of Ancient Kingdoms Amended* (published the year after Newton's death in 1727) with his own *Animadversions on Sir Isaac Newton's Book* (1728) in order to assert the historical veracity of the Bible. However, he was so impressed with Newton's method of astronomical dating that he adopted it himself and in his last book Horae Mathematicae Vacuae (1743) concluded that Jesus Christ had been born on 1 October not 25 December. Regarded as 'half crazed' by some contemporaries, he became virtually incapacitated by sciatica, died in August 1745 supposedly after falling whilst observing a comet, and was interred in the Hospital's burial ground.

When the revenue from the Kent estate recovered and another 20 boys were admitted into the school in March 1739, the Court separated the duties of Chaplain and Schoolmaster, appointing Mr Dove as full-time Schoolmaster, to teach reading, writing and arithmetic. In 1741 he was accused of neglecting his duties and left, being succeeded by George Purdy, who served until his death in 1760. The Court had decided that a Writing Master was no longer needed, but in 1742 appointed a Singing Master, Mr

THE
CHRONOLOGY
OF
ANCIENT KINGDOMS
AMENDED.

To which is Prefix'd,

A SHORT CHRONICLE *from the First Memory of Things in Europe, to the Conquest of* Persia *by* Alexander *the Great.*

By Sir ISAAC NEWTON.

LONDON:

Printed for J. TONSON in the *Strand*, and J. OSBORN and T. LONGMAN in *Pater-noster Row.*
MDCCXXVIII.

ABOVE: *The Chronology of Ancient Kingdoms.*

BELOW: *Animadversions on Sir Isaac Newton's Book.*

ANIMADVERSIONS
UPON
Sir *Isaac Newton's*
BOOK,
INTITLED
The Chronology of ancient King-doms amended.

By ARTHUR BEDFORD, *M. A.*
Rector of *Newton St. Loe* in the County of *Somerset*, and Chaplain to the *Haberdasher's Hospital* at Hoxton, near *London*.

LUKE V. 39.
No man also having drunk old wine straightway desireth new; for he faith, The old is better.

LONDON:
Printed by *Charles Ackers* in *Great-Swan-Alley*, St. *John's-street*; and Sold by R. KNAPLOCK at the *Bishop's-Head* in St. *Paul's Church-Yard*; F. FAYRAM at the *South Entrance of the Royal-Exchange*; and J. HOOKE at the *Flower-de-luce* in *Fleet-street.*
MDCCXXVIII

Hanson, to visit the Hospital once a week to teach the boys to sing the Psalms. After Bedford's death in 1745, the Court appointed the Revd Roger Shackleton Chaplain and required him to instruct the boys in their 'Moral and Religious Dutyes'. He died in office in August 1757.

Thus the school was not a grammar school teaching Latin and Greek. When the Statutes were revised in 1746 the Committee decided that the boys were to be taught only to read, write and cast-up accounts. In 1818 the Clerk to the Company told the Commission on the Education of the Children of the Poor: 'the boys are, and have always been, taught reading, writing and arithmetic. The Will does not require it to be a free grammar school, nor have the learned languages ever been taught.' When boys left at 15 (14 according to the 1746 Statutes) they were found places as apprentices, seldom as a haberdasher, but as an oil-man, fan-maker, shoemaker, bricklayer, watchmaker, pocket-book maker and gold-beater, for example.

Hogarth's *The Industrious and Idle Apprentice*, 1747.

The records contain very few references to books. In 1703 the Committee reluctantly supplied Bibles, but stipulated that in future each boy had to bring a Bible and a Prayer Book into the Hospital with him. In 1710 the Committee ordered 12 Bibles, 20 copies of Bishop Williams's A Brief Exposition of the Church Catechism and 'Tenn Grammers'. Apart from the three volumes of Foxe, and a Bible, four of the other six works mentioned in the 1733 Inventory were devotional.

Between 1739 and 1746 the Court again tried to refine the organisation and management of the Hospital. In 1739 the boys were required to attend prayers in the mornings, and from 1743 also in the afternoons. According to the 1746 Statutes, they were to have holidays on Saturday afternoons, major saints days, and a week at Christmas, Easter and Whitsuntide. In future the Court would visit the Hospital every quarter, but told the Chaplain to inspect the School once a month, and to exercise authority over the Schoolmaster, to whom it wisely also gave the liberty to make reservations to the Committee or to the Master and Wardens.

The Committee took good care of the boys' bodily and spiritual welfare. Their diet included bread and cheese for supper and half a pound of meat for dinner on 'meat days'. When the School reopened in 1739 gowns and caps were replaced with coats, waistcoats, cloth breeches and hats. After February 1740 the boys were also provided with leather breeches. In 1742 it was decided that new coats, waistcoats, cloth and leather breeches, and four shirts, were to be provided every February, new shoes three times a year, and hats every second year. Woollen socks were provided as needed.

In 1770 each boy was given a single volume published by the Society for the Propagation of the Gospel in Foreign Parts, containing a Bible, a copy of the Psalms, and the Prayer Book. The boys were allowed a wood-panelled playroom (1771), had their beds cleansed of bugs (1778, henceforth annually), received a new bathtub (1788), and were granted partitions between their beds and lockers for their clothes (1793). The Committee rarely heard from parents, but during 1765 'Samuel Petts attended this Committee and returned thanks for the education of his sons', and in 1770 Mrs Cowmeadow accused the Schoolmaster and Nurse of 'misbehaviour and ill-conduct towards her son' but the Committee concluded that they were innocent.

The Chaplains and the Schoolmasters followed the 18th-century practice of augmenting their salaries by taking private pupils. Pridie had taken day scholars, and Lovell boarders; Dove had taken private day pupils, and the Court allowed Purdy to teach up to 12 to supplement his free board and lodging plus salary of £15 a year. After Purdy's death in 1760 his successor, Edward Raine, was granted free board and lodging and only £13, but allowed 20 day boys as private pupils.

Chaplains were elected because of their connections. When Shackleton died in 1757 his successor, the Revd Michael Marlowe MA, was also from Brasenose College, Oxford, and when Marlowe retired in 1779 his successor was his son-in-law, the Revd Watts Wilkinson MA, who stayed for over 45 years. Schoolmasters usually departed a little more quickly. Edward Raine retired in 1766 to be followed by Christopher Dodd, who in 1777 was replaced by Nathaniel Catherwood, who in 1787 was succeeded by William Webb, who stayed for over 25 years.

During the 1750s the Hospital had begun to make an annual surplus of some £60, which the Company concluded 'will be more than sufficient to support and maintain and repair the buildings, notwithstanding the largeness thereof'. However, it is clear that the Company had spent too much on building the Hospital, and had invested too little to finance it. In 1775 John Entick's History of London stated 'But most of this moiety [Aske's legacy was] shamefully squandered in erecting an Edifice fitter for a Palace than an Almshouse to the great reproach of those concerned, the Company were obliged to turn off the boys for several years.'

As the Hospital aged, its maintenance became ever more expensive. In 1789 the Committee noted that it was again in bad repair, and concluded that part of the roof would have to be raised to secure the premises from rain. The Company's surveyor, John Baker, presented an annual tale of woe: cracked and loose tiles, rotten external woodwork, a hurricane in 1800, and in 1807 a fire that severely damaged the North End. In 1801 he estimated that a general repair would cost £4,000, after the fire repairs cost £1,200, and a dispute about insurance payments was not settled till 1814.

During the French Wars the price of beer, bread, butter, cheese, meat, clothes, hats, shoes, candles and coal all rose rapidly. In 1793 the brewer and in 1796 the butcher asked

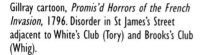

Gillray cartoon, *Promis'd Horrors of the French Invasion*, 1796. Disorder in St James's Street adjacent to White's Club (Tory) and Brooks's Club (Whig).

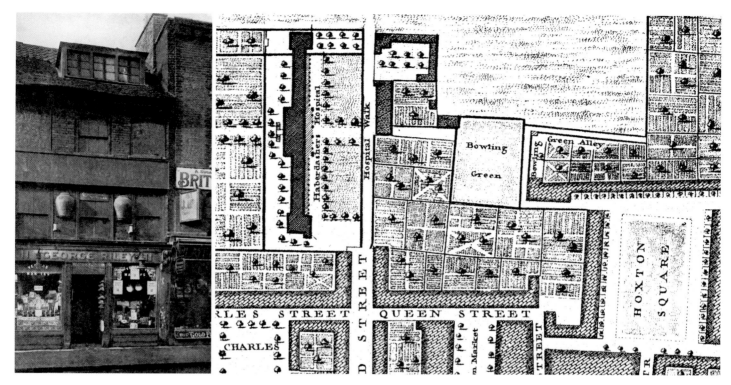

for markedly higher prices, and between 1790 and 1812 the price of 25 cauldrons of coal rose from £56 to £88. The quality of material fell, so the Committee re-awarded its contract several times in a vain attempt to find a reliable outfitter and shoemaker . In February 1800 'the scarcity of wheat' obliged it to reduce the Hospital's bread allowance, making it up with potatoes, and in November 'on account of the excessive high price of wheat and flour' it allowed the baker to replace his yearly contract with a quarterly one and agreed to relinquish its discount.

However, London's growth provided financial opportunities. In 1791 the Committee reviewed the state of the Hospital, and in 1792 Baker prepared a detailed plan of the Hospital itself and of the Hoxton estate, and proposed to grant building leases. Development began in 1802. There were numerous problems. In 1811 Baker complained that one builder was running up houses of such low quality that the district would be turned into a slum inhabited by thugs and whores, a prediction that very nearly came true by the end of the century. Fortunately, from 1806 onwards the estate yielded an annual surplus that was invested and put towards a fund to repair or rebuild the Hospital. (The first road to be laid out, Haberdasher Street, still exists, as do several later roads, often named after parts of the Kent estate, for example Ashford, Buttesland and Chart Streets.)

ABOVE, CLOCKWISE FROM LEFT: A shop in Pitfield Street, 1922.

Haberdashers' Hospital on Rocque's map of London and Westminster, 1746.

Nineteenth-century house in Buttesland Street today, to the immediate north of the Hospital.

The Hospital as rebuilt, 1824–26.

3

Rebuilding and Reform

1813–1868

The boys had often been in trouble for theft, but in 1813 they tried arson. On Sunday 4 April a small fire was discovered and quickly put out. Next day the loft stairs were found well alight, but the Hospital was saved when the Matron, Nurse and some of the pensioners doused the flames. On Tuesday 6 a boy named Wessells confessed that he had started the fire so that he would be sent home to his mother – so the Committee suspended him and sent him home! Re-interrogated four days later, he implicated other boys, and after the Schoolmaster, the Matron, the Nurse and the Company's Clerk had questioned all the boys it appeared that Dawson, Freeman, Gibbs and Lessingham had helped him, and that eight other boys knew what was afoot. All had hoped to be sent home. The ringleaders were expelled and the lesser eight flogged. They were lucky not to forfeit the 6d. given to each boy on Aske's birthday, an additional penalty usually imposed for serious misdemeanours.

Shocked by the boys' attempted arson, in May 1813 the Court set up a Select Committee to examine the management of the Hospital. It made an unannounced visit, sampled what was being served at dinner, and reviewed the weekly diet. For pensioners and boys it was replete with beer (the boys had half a pint with each meal), bread, butter, cheese, potatoes and meat (boiled, roast and stewed), with greens at dinner on Wednesdays. It concentrated on the accounts. In 1812 the Hospital had made a loss of £206, but the Committee estimated that during 1813 increased rents from the Kent and Hoxton estates would produce additional income of £436 for the year, resulting in a surplus of £230 to be added to the fund, then standing at £3,500.

That progress was timely. In 1818 the Master, Wardens, Clerk and Schoolmaster were summoned to the Commissioners on the Education of the Children of the Poor, and told to bring all the accounts and documents relating to the Hospital. It was a chastening experience. The Commissioners' report was critical. It found that the original and the current measured area of the Kent estate differed by over 27 acres, and that the Company had confused its own and the charity's accounts. Thus the Company believed it was owed over £7,000 by the charity, but in fact the Company owed over £900 to the charity (solving the mystery of the money unaccounted for in the 1690s). It concluded that the confusion had contributed to the charity's financial difficulties, and demanded that the situation be clarified.

The Company then examined the Hospital again. In 1821 its new Surveyor, Mr Spiller, recommended extensive redecoration, renovation and reconstruction at an estimated cost of £6,830. Benjamin Hawes (fourth Warden in 1818 and Master in 1831) took the initiative and in February 1823 a Special Committee decided to rebuild according to a 'Plain Grecian' design by D.R. Roper, a London architect, who estimated the building cost at £12,097. The site was vacated by Christmas, and the demolition men and builders took possession. The Chaplain was given a £120 living out allowance, the pensioners £1 a week each, and the boys moved to a nearby house. The old Hospital was quickly demolished, the foundation stone of the new one laid on 31 May 1824 and the new premises declared complete on 23 June 1826.

Aske's statue was brought down from the pediment, but was found to be badly damaged and so was discarded, a Coade Stone replacement being set on an inscribed plinth in the centre of the new courtyard. A central block with a massive Doric portico

Rebuilt Hospital showing alms houses to north and south.

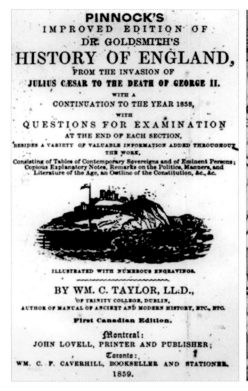

The persons of pronouns are three in each number, viz.

I, is the first person
Thou, is the second person   } Singular.
He, she, or *it,* is the third person

We, is the first person
Ye, or *you,* is the second person   } Plural.
They, is the third person

This account of persons will be very intelligible, when we reflect, that there are three persons who may be the subject of any discourse: first, the person who speaks, may speak of himself; secondly, he may speak of the person to whom he addresses himself; thirdly, he may speak of some other person: and as the speakers, the persons spoken to, and the other persons spoken of, may be many, so each of these persons must have the plural number.

The Numbers of pronouns, like those of substantives, are two, the singular and the plural: as, *I, thou, he; we, ye* or *you, they.*

Gender has respect only to the third person singular of the pronouns, *he, she, it. He* is masculine; *she* is feminine; *it* is neuter.

The persons speaking and spoken to, being at the same time the subjects of the discourse, are supposed to be present; from which, and other circumstances, their sex is commonly known, and needs not to be marked by a dis-

ABOVE: Textbooks used in the School in the late 1820s, FROM LEFT: Oliver Goldsmith's *History of England, Aesop's Fables* and Lindley Murray's *Grammar.*

BELOW: Lindley Murray.

facing east contained the chapel, dining room and school room on the ground floor, the boys' dormitory and Matron's quarters on the first floor, domestic quarters in the basement, and accommodation for the Chaplain (a spacious house) and Schoolmaster (in the basement). To the north and south were almshouses for the pensioners. The east side was still separated from Pitfield Street by iron railings. The complex was more compact than the old site, allowing the Company to lay out four streets containing 275 houses whose ground rents added to the Hospital's income.

The Committee made every effort to ensure that the new Hospital flourished. It appointed a new Chaplain (the Revd Charles Davies) and employed an entirely new domestic staff. Only the Schoolmaster, George Hamilton, originally appointed in 1820, survived from the previous Hospital, probably because he had been educated in the school and been made a Liveryman of the company. The Committee bought new fixtures and fittings (including ten iron double bedsteads for the boys, 'made extra strong'), supervised cleaning, decorating and equipping the premises, established a weekly cycle of meals, and issued revised Statutes and school rules.

Every 24 February, Aske's birthday, the boys took an oral exam, and the most proficient were presented with books as prizes. The Head Boy recited a set speech to commemorate Aske's munificence, for which he received 5/-, and the other boys were given 1/- each. In summer, they studied from 6 to 8 a.m., from 9 a.m. to 12 noon, and from 2 to 5 p.m., a long day. Their textbooks were Lindley Murray's *Grammar,* Oliver Goldsmith's *History of England, Aesop's Fables* and Enfield's *Speaker.* They were not to enter the kitchen or to run errands, but on half-holidays the schoolmaster was to take them for a healthy walk. They were to be seen to bed at night not by the maids, as before, but by the Porter.

The overall estimate for the new Hospital had been £13,455, but the eventual total cost, including architect's fees and fittings, was £18,881, far larger than the £7,188 building fund, and the Company had borrowed most of the difference. Yet in 1826 the Committee raised all salaries and allowances (the Schoolmaster's salary rose from £30 to £52). By 1829/30 there was a £500 deficit. In October 1830 a Special Committee appointed to investigate found that the Chaplain had committed misconduct with a maidservant and noted 'the great insubordination in the school and the disorganized state of the establishment'. An interpolation (in red ink) in the full Committee's minutes records that on 30 October 1830 'The establishment was closed and the boys sent home to 8 April 1831.'

After demanding drastic economies the Committee proposed to grant a new Chaplain £700 a year to teach the boys with the help of an Usher (assistant teacher), and to manage all domestic aspects of the Hospital hitherto dealt with by the Committee. In February 1831 it appointed the Revd John Laming Turner, and in April he engaged Mr Townsend as Usher at £30 a year. In May 1832 the system was judged a success. Turner had overspent by £48, but the Committee raised his grant to £800 and minuted 'the boys are much better educated and maintained than under the former system'.

However, the less of the £800 Turner spent, the greater was his income. In 1842 the Committee found that he did not provide the weekly diet set in 1831, ordered him to offer the boys a choice of beer or water with meals, and urged the Company to provide them with single beds, as did the Visitation Committee, citing reasons of 'propriety'. In 1836 Hawes had not objected to the boys sleeping two to a bed but considered 'excellent feather beds' were too luxurious for them and would unfit them for their future lowly position in society. Not until 1845, when four boys were expelled and six severely reprimanded, did the full Committee demand that single beds be provided 'immediately'. Even then they were not supplied till 1848 when Turner complained of the cost of buying and washing ten extra pairs of sheets.

In 1831 Turner had been contracted to instruct the boys in 'Reading, writing, arithmetic, the English Grammar, Latin Accidence, Geography, and the elements of Mathematics and Merchants' Accounts', the Usher to specialise in teaching writing and arithmetic. In 1832 the Committee had been impressed, but in 1834 Hawes proposed that 'some competent person' be engaged to examine the boys in the Company's Hall just before the summer and winter holidays. The Committee duly appointed the Revd Thomas Grose MA, formerly of Clare College, Cambridge, and in December 1835 he held the first of many half-yearly oral examinations.

The Committee had to decide what was to be taught and to ensure that it was well taught. In 1849 it wanted advice on 'the most beneficial education to be given to the class of boys to be admitted' and consulted the Revd Dr F.W. Mortimer, Headmaster of the City of London School. Early in 1850 he suggested that Latin grammar be abandoned and replaced by Technical Drawing and French, subjects more appropriate for 'boys intended for business' and more 'likely to be advantageous to such boys in later life'. He thought that the school's textbooks needed updating, for example abandoning Goldsmith's *History of England* (1771) and adopting the Revd J.W. Colenso's *Arithmetic for Schools* (1843), and recommended that teaching should be the responsibility not of the Chaplain but of a qualified Schoolmaster.

In November 1850 Mr Carterfield ('his attainments are adequate') was appointed the new Usher at £50 a year plus free board and lodging, but in 1852 the Committee responded to further complaints against Turner by restructuring the school. It revised the Statutes, banned private pupils, introduced an extra lesson on each weekday evening, and put the boys into a uniform of dark jacket and 'pepper and salt' trousers. Turner was relegated to the position of Chaplain at £150 a year and Carterfield was appointed Schoolmaster with a salary of £100 plus a house. After further complaints, in 1854 Turner was dismissed and the Revd Alfred Jones appointed Chaplain.

In 1858 Dr Mortimer found that French had been introduced but Latin grammar was still being taught and Goldsmith was still being used, and recommended that geometry, mechanics and natural philosophy (science) should be taught. Carterfield's response was unimpressive and a vote of censure on his conduct and record moved by Hawes failed by only six votes to five. During January 1862 the Court asked the Committee to consider altering and improving the half-yearly exams. Hawes wanted to make 'the education of the Scholars more useful to them and better adapted to their probable future positions in life' by giving more time to the basic subjects of 'English composition, writing from dictation, physical geography and practical mechanics'.

A devout and pious evangelical, Jones devoted most of his first ten years to the pensioners, as he put it in an 'endeavour to win their souls for Christ'. He also gave the boys a series of lectures on the Bible, provided religious instruction for an hour every Sunday morning, introduced divinity exams, set up a small library of religious tracts, including his own book on the proper names of the Old Testament, and tried to ensure that they took an active part in the weekday and Sunday chapel services as Bible readers and singers.

The boys reacted against this spiritual discipline. In November 1855 and July 1856 the Master of the Company reproved them for misbehaving in chapel. After similar incidents in 1864 they complained to the Committee that prayers took up too much of their time. The Monitor (Head Boy) told Jones about further misbehaviour and he reported to the Committee 'that while I was putting on my robes before the service, Vokins [one of the boys] was within the Communion rails, and went through a mock ceremony of devotion'.

During March 1864 Arthur Donne ran away and was brought back in the early hours of the morning by a policeman, and on 14 April the Master discovered that he and four other boys had been sneaking through an unlocked door in the basement and spending their evenings in the West End. When the Master called an emergency meeting of the Committee on 21 April it found that two boys had run away and were with their parents at home. Several boys were expelled and Carterfield was dismissed without a pension. In January 1865 Jones was designated both Chaplain and Headmaster, and Thomas Kimber was appointed Second Master, a position which still exists.

The Committee redoubled its interest in the school and after its quarterly meeting called the boys into the Court Room after lunch and gave them 1/- each, except for the

Revd Dr F.W. Mortimer, Headmaster of the City of London School.

A school master with his pupils, 1860s.

Monitor who got 2/6d. Jones relaxed his spiritual discipline, inviting the boys to tea with his family on Sunday afternoons. He arranged occasional trips to Epping Forest and to the permanent home of the Crystal Palace in Sydenham, and ensured that they had a weekly half holiday in Victoria Park or on Hackney Downs. He reorganised their education, devised a system of December and June exams with separate papers in each subject, introduced weekly tests ('I know exactly how each boy is doing in his work'), and compared marks from one year to the next. He added books on chemistry, geology and mechanics to the school library. The Company provided prizes for freehand drawing and natural philosophy(science), then a rarity in any school.

The academic standard is hard to assess. Kimber taught all 20 boys, aged from nine to fifteen, in one schoolroom, and two visiting teachers taught drawing and French. Jones's reports to the Committee overestimated the boys' achievement. In the June 1865 exam the boys' trigonometry was judged 'a failure' and they were 'very imperfect' in their knowledge of the geography and history of England. In December 1867 the Committee therefore appointed a new examiner, Joseph Harris MA, assistant master at the City of London School, who concluded that the boys tried to learn their lessons by heart without thinking about them or understanding them, so in 1871 he persuaded the Committee to replace the half-yearly examinations with a demanding yearly exam.

By then relations between Jones and Kimber were breaking down. In January 1865 Jones had reported 'Mr Kimber I believe to be a superior schoolmaster. He is most kind and attentive to the boys, but will allow no irregularities.' By May Jones had his doubts, since Kimber refused to accept his advice on a number of issues. Jones later accused Kimber of allowing the boys' reading and writing to decline, deputing their half-day walk to the gatekeeper, being absent from Sunday chapel, and frequently staying out at night instead of doing his duty. On 26 February 1872 he recorded, 'The scholars have frequently complained to me about Mr Kimber striking them with a long stick. I have spoken to him about it: but I am sorry to say, that he has been using it freely this morning, and has cut Breeze across his face. He has also hit the Monitor several times on the face. Breeze will carry the mark on his face home with him today. I do not find any reason for it, even if he had authority to use the stick.'

Hitherto the school had been virtually isolated from national trends in education. In 1864 the government set up the Taunton Commission on endowed schools, a type that included Aske's Hospital. The Charity Commissioners had reviewed the Hospital in 1862 as part of their report into the City of London Livery Companies, but the Taunton Commissioners had greater influence. After making an initial visit to the Hospital in 1864, they wrote to the Company in July 1866 suggesting that the charity's increased income gave an opportunity to 'enlarge and invigorate its working' and asked the Company to state its intentions.

When in 1866 the Taunton Commission made its second visit to Hoxton it found that the boys still studied Latin, but approved of their French, Euclid (geometry) and algebra. However, it remarked dismissively that Aske's Hospital pupils were the sons of 'Widows, trades people, etc.', and implied that the charity's income of some £4,000 was capable of maintaining far more than 20 pensioners and a school for 20 boarders. Indeed, the Commission had found that Manchester Grammar School used an income of £2,994 to provide 250 entirely free places for day pupils.

The Company calculated that the Charity's income was about £5,000 a year and estimated that by 1885 it would be about £12,000 so considered two plans. The Charities Committee proposed to admit ten more boarders and 50 day pupils at Hoxton. The Estates Committee argued that 'Hoxton is not one of [London's] most favoured localities and experience shows that there is seldom a boy in the school whose parents reside in Hoxton' so suggested building a boarding and day school on land owned by the William Jones Charity in Hatcham. Anxious to follow the terms of Aske's will, it proposed to limit admission at Hoxton to the sons of Liverymen and Freemen, and to give preference to them at Hatcham, so rejected the Hoxton Middle Class Education Committee's request to admit local residents' sons as day pupils.

After initially favouring the Charity Committee's proposal, in November 1868 the Court accepted the Estates Committee's plan.

4

Reconstitution at Hoxton

1868–1898

Published in 1868, the Taunton Report considered that hospital schools had the merit of lifting their pupils out of the labouring class, but that their educational standards suffered from the absence of entrance exams, of adequate internal exams, and of day pupils. It proposed to found English secondary education on a system of first, second and third grade schools: 'The most urgent educational need of the country is for good schools of the third grade.' They would cater for the children of artisans and small shopkeepers by charging fees of no more than £4 a year. They would teach 'modern' subjects to pupils who were to leave by the end of the term in which they were 14, equipped at least with 'a clerk's education, namely, a thorough knowledge of arithmetic, and the ability to write a good letter'.

In response to the Taunton Report, in 1869 the Endowed Schools Act established the Endowed Schools Commission, which was charged with supervising and if necessary reorganising charitable trusts which supported endowed schools, besides widening the educational opportunities open to girls. The Commission was unimpressed by the Company's plans to restrict the benefits of the Charity to the sons of its own members and demanded that it submit a new 'Scheme'. The Company then added a day school for 100 boys in Hoxton to its proposed day and boarding school at Hatcham. In February 1870 the Court received a letter of rejection from the Commission's secretary, H.J. Roby, outlining a very different educational philosophy: a good school was one with an entrance exam open to all comers, with 'exhibitions on a liberal scale so as to give the most promising boys an

The School Boys' and Masters' Cricket XI, 1890s. R.W. Hinton, Headmaster, sporting his characteristic white waistcoat, middle back row.

ABOVE: R.W. Hinton, Headmaster 1875–1909.

Prize Day Programme, 1889.

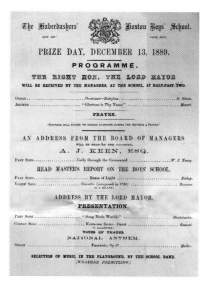

opportunity of rising into the rank for which their natural gifts fit them'. That was a vision of Haberdashers' future.

In December 1870 the Company set up an Endowed Schools Committee, and after difficult and prolonged negotiations a final Scheme was agreed on 5 April 1873 and embodied in an Order in Council that Queen Victoria signed at Osborne House in August. It was for a day school for 300 boys and another for 300 girls at Hoxton, and one for 300 boys and another for 200 girls at Hatcham, but all four schools were to have a single governing body. As Foundation Governors, the Company retained ownership of the Hoxton and Kent estates, and nominated nine members of the Board of Managers (two of whom had to be women), whilst the other six were appointed by the Lord Mayor and Aldermen, Common Council and the Greenwich and Hackney School Boards, the latter of which appointed Sir Charles Reid, a Liberal MP. The schools could award Entrance Exhibitions to the sons and grandsons of Freemen, but half of the schools' other Entrance Exhibitions were reserved for pupils from elementary schools, run either by the School Boards or the various churches.

At Hoxton changes were dramatic. During 1874 Jones, Kimber and the 20 old men were pensioned off, and most of the 20 boys sent to a boarding school in Margate. The school closed on 24 June. Meeting for the first time on 16 December 1873, the Managers had found that there was not enough money for four separate schools. The Company's architect, William Snook, estimated that two new schools at Hoxton would cost £12,000, but the Endowed Schools Commissioners had set a limit of £5,000, so the Almshouses were demolished and the central block of Roper's buildings was adapted for a Girls' School and a Boys' School at opposite ends. The old chapel was remodelled as a shared assembly hall, from 1876 containing a portrait of Robert Aske lent by the Company. The Duke of Connaught, Queen Victoria's third son, an honorary Liveryman, opened the schools on 5 June 1875, for some years afterwards regarded as Founder's Day. The new Headmaster of the Boys' School was Mr R.W. Hinton BA. Born in 1843, he had graduated from London University in 1872, and was assistant science and art master at the London Orphanage Asylum, Watford. (Near Watford Junction Railway Station, it has been converted into flats.)

According to the 1873 Scheme, the Haberdashers' Boys' School, Hoxton, was to give 'sound, practical and liberal education'. Fees were to be £2–£4 a year and pupils were to leave by the end of the term in which they were 15. In other words, it was to be a superior sort of third grade school, whereas the Hatcham schools were intended to be second grade schools, of a higher standard and status. In contrast to many schools of the time, corporal punishment was to be used 'as seldom as possible'. It advertised itself as a 'middle class day school' which taught 'reading and spelling, arithmetic and elementary mathematics, English grammar, composition and literature, history, political and physical geography, natural science, Latin or French or both, drawing and vocal music'. Drill and gymnastics, geometrical and mechanic drawing, book-keeping and shorthand were soon added. Carpentry, German (an alternative to Latin), instrumental music, and painting were available as optional extras.

Most applicants took an entrance exam in January, as they still do. Boys entered the preparatory form at eight or nine, and the main school at 10 or 11, or at 11 or 12 from elementary schools. In 1885 18 of the 36 entrants were poor children from elementary schools who held Entrance Exhibitions. 16 of the 24 boys in the sixth form, whose average age was 15.3, were helped by Exhibitions. Leavers took the City and Guilds, College of Preceptors, Department of Science and Art and Cambridge Local examinations, and were eligible for Leaving Exhibitions. The two schools shared £400 for Entrance and £600 for Leaving Exhibitions each year, the former to a maximum of £12 each.

The Boys' School was a very competitive place, as surviving lists of Entrance, School and Leaving Exhibitions make clear. The first pupil to win a university degree was F.G. Pepper, nicknamed 'Mr Hinton's boy', who had stayed on as a pupil teacher, and in 1889 was awarded a London BA, in the same year changing his name to F.G. Russell as if to emphasise his new status. The first to go to Cambridge was R.T. Smith who in 1892 graduated with a first-class degree in mathematics, having entered St John's via Finsbury Technical College. Similarly, the first to go to Oxford was F.W. Hinton, one of the Headmaster's two sons, who in 1894 won an open scholarship at St John's to read classics, via Merchant Taylors' School.

The school flourished, its low fees and 'modern' syllabus attracting fee-payers and Exhibitioners from all over London. In 1886 it had 413 pupils. Hours were from 9 to 12.30

Boys and Masters on steps of the Hoxton School, 1891.

Details of the Hoxton School in 2007, now converted into apartments for high-earning City workers.

a.m., and from 2 to 4 p.m., with half holidays on Wednesday and Saturday afternoons. Four weeks holiday was given in the summer, three weeks at Christmas and one week at Easter. Commendation Day at the end of the Autumn Term was a major social event. Facilities for teaching chemistry and physics had not been provided in 1873, but from 1876 were subsidised by the Department of Science and Art, and from 1894 by the London County Council's Technical Education Board, in return for LCC-appointed managers. In 1882 the premises were remodelled and in 1883 boys allowed to stay until they were 17, although few did so (in 1895 only nine were over 16). The school developed many extra-curricular activities. During the Autumn Term of 1883 a short-lived school magazine serialised a ghost story by F.G. Pepper, then still a student teacher. By 1885 the school gave an annual concert, had a band, cricket and swimming clubs, a weather recording unit, a savings bank, a museum and a library. Founder's Day sports were held in Tufnell Park.

However, by the late 1880s there were signs of trouble ahead. The British economy was in recession. The London School Board had begun to provide a similar but cheaper education in its Higher Grade Schools. The neighbourhood had deteriorated. Charles Booth, the pioneer of social surveys, called Hoxton 'the principal criminal quarter in London'. The boys' starched white Eton collars and dark jackets aroused the animosity of slum children in the streets. In May 1889 Miss Millar, Headmistress of the Girls' School, proposed to protect her girls from the 'unseemly behaviour' of 'street toughs', and reverse her school's falling numbers, by moving it to the northern suburbs where most of the girls lived. By 1892 she had the support of the Managers, the Company, and the Headmaster of the Boys' School.

In March 1893 the Charity Commissioners agreed. They concluded that 'the poorer classes' living nearby could not afford the fees. They found that the pupils' parents were mostly clerks, shopkeepers and commercial travellers, mainly living in Hornsey, Wood Green and Tottenham, but with a fair proportion from Clapton, Leyton and Islington. Thus only 17% of pupils lived within one mile of the schools, but 17% lived more than five miles away, enduring a long and time-consuming daily journey either on foot or by public transport in order to acquire a good education.

The school's academic standard is less easy to judge. Classes were large. In 1886, when the school had 12 teachers and 413 boys, only three of the ten forms contained fewer than 40 boys, six from 40 to 50 inclusive, and the largest 59 (its tuition being shared with a pupil-teacher). Reports of external oral examinations carried out between 1887 and 1902 are too general to be informative. In 1896 and 1897 an inspector reporting on behalf of the Senate of London University confirmed the school's own view: 'This is essentially a

The Sixth Form (average age 15), R.W. Hinton left front, and the School's four graduate masters, left to right; Stokes, Russell, Woodcock and Batcheldor, 1894.

Modern school, attention being given mainly to Mathematics, English (including Book-keeping and Short-hand) and Science'. The facilities for chemistry and physics were still judged to be inadequate. Languages were taught only to the top two forms in terms of age; French being adequate, German unsatisfactory and Latin largely elementary. Despite that chequered verdict, the school contained some brilliant boys determined to make their way in the world.

In 1893 R.T. Smith had been appointed Professor of Science at the University of Cape Colony, and in 1903 H.W. Waynforth (his contemporary) was Professor of Engineering at King's College, London. H.R. Dent had joined his family firm and taken charge of publishing *Everyman's Encyclopaedia* and the innovative *Everyman* books. A further literary connection was provided by George and Charles Foyle, who ran businesses of their own, and whose younger brothers were proprietors of the famous bookshop in Charing Cross Road. (George's grandson, Alan H. Roberts, was a pupil at Haberdashers'

Tennis, 1890s. R.W. Hinton, Headmaster, front left.

ABOVE: The Sydney Harbour Bridge, designed by Sir Ralph Freeman, (BELOW).

in the 1950s.) Harold Downer, a pupil-teacher during 1887/88, was well on his way to becoming an influential City solicitor, who served as Alderman, Magistrate and Sheriff, and was knighted as Lord Mayor Elect for 1937 but died before assuming office.

The most brilliant boy of the time was probably Ralph Freeman, the third son of George James Freeman, a prosperous Hoxton tobacconist and cigar and cigarette maker, who sent each of his six sons to Haberdashers', and was later instrumental in establishing the Imperial Tobacco Company. Born in 1880, Ralph joined Haberdashers' in 1888 and in 1897 left for the Central Technical College in South Kensington, where he won the three most prestigious awards, the Institute and Samuel scholarships and the Siemens medal. Four years later he joined Sir Douglas Fox & Partners, consulting engineers, and had a remarkable career as a civil engineer. In the early 1920s he designed the Sydney Harbour Bridge, when it was opened in 1932 the world's heaviest and longest single span bridge, and during both world wars did work of the utmost national importance. He was knighted in 1947 and died in 1950.

Unfortunately, suitable sites for a new school were scarce. The Charity Commissioners quibbled about which district most needed new schools. The uncertainty unsettled parents, so applications declined, boys left the school, and numbers fell. The Company wanted to sell the Hoxton site for building to raise money to finance the new schools, but the LCC and the Charity Commissioners insisted that the buildings were used for education and that the front court remained an open space. The LCC was thus the only buyer and in 1895 the Company agreed to its final offer of £21,000. The Company then had a fund of £57,000, and the Charity's net income for the year was a substantial £13,830. In May 1897 the Company paid £6,500 for five acres in West Hampstead, leaving £24,156 for building, and £26,444 for the Girls' School, which found a site in West Acton. However, the LCC insisted on taking possession of the Hoxton site in June 1898, so the Managers had to find temporary premises for the Boys' School and leased two houses, Elm Lodge and Wood Brook. They were near to the site on which the new school was to be built in Westbere Road, then a muddy cul-de-sac ending in fields, but on the edge of the prosperous suburban area in which the school was to establish itself and flourish.

5

Expansion at Hampstead

1898–1920

The Managers had planned a three-storey building with an extensive basement, the whole including nine general classrooms, an art room, two science rooms and a lecture theatre, a dining room and assembly hall, with an adjacent gymnasium and swimming pool, the latter capable of being boarded over and used as a carpenter's shop in winter. However, the Boer War caused prices to rise so rapidly that the lowest tender was £25,861, so during the autumn of 1899 the Charity Commissioners demanded that the plans be revised and the building scaled down, so it could be completed within the original estimate of £23,000. Henry Stock, the Company's new architect, cut back on the most expensive individual elements, including the art room, chemistry laboratory, lecture theatre and cloakrooms. The Commissioners did not grant a new Scheme until 12 November 1900, and a building contract was not finally signed until March 1901. The boys moved in during September 1902 and although not yet fully equipped the school was opened on 13 January 1903. At the end of term the form captains presented Hinton with a vote of thanks signed by every boy and master, plus a solid-silver tea and coffee set, to mark their gratitude for the achievement.

The LCC converted the Hoxton building into the Shoreditch Technical Institute, and it remained a technical college for many years, although it has recently been converted into apartments and flats as parts of Hoxton have been redeveloped. D.R. Roper's Doric portico and Grecian façade survive intact, bearing inscriptions placed there in the 1820s and 1870s, still facing across a grassed and railed court onto Pitfield Street. The schools retained some mementoes of the years

Class 1B, 1913. Photo donated by Edward Mautner,
third on left (wearing spectacles).

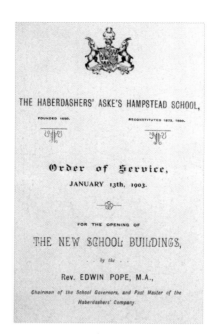

ABOVE: Order of Service for opening the Hampstead School, 1903.

BELOW, LEFT TO RIGHT: School certificate, front cover of the first *Skylark*, Scheme of Terms and Holidays, Book plate.

before 1903. Robert Aske's statue was sent to Hatcham, the table used by the boys in the Dining Hall in 1697 was placed in the Masters' Common Room at Hampstead, the Communion Table from the original Chapel was placed on the assembly hall platform, and a stone carving of the Company's coat of arms was transferred to the façade of the new building.

The Managers (designated Governors in 1900) had sacked most of the masters in 1898, so only Hinton, Russell and Stokes (since 1876 Sixth Form and Second Master) survived the move to Hampstead. Only 96 boys transferred to Hampstead and only six of them remained in 1903, outnumbered by 312 new boys. According to the new Scheme, the school remained a 'modern' one, teaching 'commercial subjects' as a matter of course and Greek only as an optional extra, but in many ways the school was entirely new, in terms of the Taunton Report a second grade school. Saturday morning lessons were no more. Fees were set in the range of £4 to £8 a year and boys were able to remain to 18 with special permission. The London County Council and Middlesex County Council each had the right to nominate Governors. Despite its unwieldy full name, the Haberdashers' Aske's Hampstead Boys' School was destined for success.

Hinton, known to the boys as 'Soccar', in allusion to the ancient Greek philosopher Socrates, recruited more graduate teachers, and modified the practice of teaching all subjects in form groups. The school certainly impressed parents. Designed for 300 boys, applications were buoyant, and by the end of 1905 it had 412 pupils. The first number of *Skylark*, the school magazine, was issued in the Spring Term of 1903, its title a reference to the school's then semi-rural surroundings, so different from the smoky environs of Hoxton, and recorded the school's rapid evolution as, in the terminology of 100 years later, it rebranded itself and went upmarket.

During 1905 the school adopted an official hymn, a prayer and a psalm, and a school song – *Forward, Straight Forward* – composed and set to music by Russell. Later in the year the Governors gave £100 for a reference library and Hinton designed a book-plate encapsulating the school's history: Give Arts. Give Aid (said to be Aske's motto) was

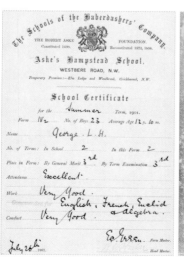

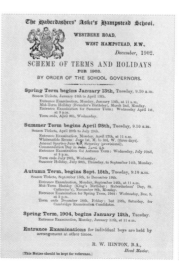

School Hall at Hampstead, c.1910.

printed with 'Keep Time and Tune' (the Hoxton motto, derived from the clock and organ in the hall) and 'Serve and Obey' (the Company's motto, which the school adopted as its own).

Education legislation had recently changed. The 1902 Education Act designated county and county borough councils as local education authorities (LEAs) and allowed them to use rate aid to promote secondary education, subject to inspection and 'recognition' by the Board of Education. The 1903 Government of London Act abolished the London School Board, and gave its powers of inspection to the LCC, within whose boundaries the school lay. Relying on a report from the LCC, which referred to Haberdashers' as 'this excellent school', the Board recognised the school during 1905, and sent in its Chief Inspector during March 1906. His report criticised the decoration, equipment, number, situation and size of the classrooms, and other facilities (including the cloakrooms), besides declaring that class sizes were too large, the boys inadequately assessed and graded by ability, and the school overcrowded. It noted that although most subjects were taught to form groups of mixed ability, rather than in sets, the 20 masters (two-thirds of whom were graduates) were 'good and conscientious' and gave 'some remarkably good teaching'. It concluded: 'the school should have a long and successful future before it'.

After receiving a copy, the LCC sent in its own Chief Inspector in December 1906. He believed that the classrooms 'compare favourably with many classrooms in our London schools' and found slightly less overcrowding. Under pressure from the Board of Education, the school had reduced the number of boys from 412 to 364, and employed an extra master (but only three out of 11 forms had fewer than 30 boys). The 'underpaid' but 'keen and energetic' teaching staff (now reduced to 19), who included 12 graduates, were hampered by the fact that setting was as yet limited to art, carpentry and science. The LCC report noted that parents valued the school, and recommended adopting setting in all subjects, reapportioning the Charity's income in favour of Hampstead and starting an immediate building programme.

Stone coat arms, moved from the Hoxton School to Hampstead.

The Governors turned the new legislation and the 1906 reports to the school's advantage. In 1905 the school received £360 from the LCC, a significant proportion of the total income of £5,821 (the balance made up of £4,569 in fees and £892 from the Charity). Under the terms of the 1907 Education (Administrative Provisions) Act, in return for offering 12.5% of the places in the school to pupils from public elementary schools aged 12 and over, whose fees would be paid by the LEAs, the school would receive a £5 per year capitation grant for every pupil in that age group, whether an LEA pupil or a private fee-payer. In 1908 work therefore began on a new wing, which was opened on 27 April 1909. The ground floor of the 'old' wing accommodated dining hall and kitchen, library and preparatory department, and cloak rooms and lavatories; its first floor contained assembly hall, the Headmaster's study and masters' common room, and general classrooms; and its upper floor housed chemistry and physics laboratories and a lecture theatre; whilst the 'new' wing boasted a new art room, a swimming bath, a workshop for manual training (carpentry) and a gymnasium.

Within a year the number of boys rose to 498, and during the financial year 1910/11 the school received £1,285 as a result of 257 boys qualifying for £5 grants from the Board of Education. Unfortunately, Hinton's health had failed (he had turned 65 in 1908) so he prepared to retire. He took his leave of the school on 28 July 1909 when over one thousand boys, old boys, parents and staff gathered to make a presentation to him and his wife, the largest and warmest display of affection and respect for any Haberdashers' Headmaster. The Board's 1906 report had recognised his achievement: 'He is entirely devoted to the school and the success that has attended it, in spite of trying changes, is due very largely to his untiring energy, and to his knowledgeable and careful supervision of every detail connected with the school.'

BELOW: Swimming pool at Hampstead.

FACING PAGE, TOP: First surviving photo of the whole School at Hampstead.

Hinton was a man of his time. He spent his last full day as Headmaster with the Haberdashers' Cadets at Bisley. He advised the boys to develop character and to base it on morality, religion and revelation. He did not long survive his retirement and died of rheumatic fever and bronchitis on 9 May 1912. His obituary in *Skylark* recorded his kindness and consideration to the boys, his interest in the old boys and their careers, his accessibility to parents, and his sincere friendship for his colleagues. Hinton also supported the wider school community, fostering the Old Boys' Club (established in 1888, since 1964 the Old Haberdashers' Association), and helping to found the Old Boys' Lodge of Freemasons, No. 3362 (set up in 1909). Both retain close links with the school. (A memorial plaque to Hinton from the assembly hall at Hampstead is in Aldenham House Waiting Room, next to the First War Memorial.) In Hinton's day the Hampstead school gave mainly middle class boys the chance to rise through the social hierarchy of the time. In 1906 the Board of Education report noted that only 21 (*c.* 5%) of the school's 412 pupils were from working-class backgrounds. In 1908 a report by the University of London stated:

> The boys are well-behaved and work hard. The average level of intelligence is high, as one might expect from the class to which they belong. They are devoted to their school and grateful for the excellent opportunities which it offers them.

The honours boards and lists of old boys' achievements in the Headmaster's annual report show that after they left school many boys took professional examinations, becoming accountants, actuaries, architects, barristers, dentists, doctors, engineers, solicitors, surgeons, etc.

BELOW: The School's first Honours Board, 1876–1905.

Mrs Edith Freeman.

As was the custom of the day, very few even of the ablest pupils went to university. For example, Ralph Freeman's three younger brothers were amongst the six pupils who transferred from Hoxton to Hampstead, to which all six brothers donated the House Cricket Shield in 1904, but only one of them studied at a university. Arnold was School Captain in 1903/04, Captain of cricket and soccer, the leading scholar in the school, and entered St John's College, Oxford, but forsook a legal career to devote himself to social work. Peter founded the Debating Society and in 1929 won Brecon and Radnor for Labour, giving Haberdashers' its first MP. Frank won the school's Bronze Medal for all-round excellence and became a distinguished architect. (Their mother, Mrs Edith Marion Freeman, celebrated her 100th birthday on 24 January 1952, an event celebrated by a portrait in *Skylark*.)

Hinton was succeeded by A.J. Spilsbury. He was an able man (School Captain of Christ's Hospital, Scholar of Queen's College, Oxford, a classicist and an archaeologist) and an experienced teacher (having taught at Brecon College, Brighton College, and the City of London School, where he was Senior Classical Master and commanded the Officers' Training Corps) but he suffered a breakdown and resigned before the end of the Autumn Term. However, Spilsbury made a complete recovery and in 1917 became the Headmaster of Queen Elizabeth Grammar School, Wakefield. (Spilsbury's portrait hangs in the Old Refectory in Aldenham House, together with those of the other Headmasters since 1875.)

In January 1910 his successor, C.J.L. Wagstaff, arrived from Oundle, a boarding school known for its science teaching. Wagstaff, formerly a Scholar of Emmanuel College, Cambridge, had first class degrees in Mathematics and Natural Science, was the author of science textbooks, and had taught at Bradford Grammar School before moving to Oundle. Under his guidance Haberdashers' became a first grade school, a type that the Taunton Report had suggested might one day rival the great public schools. In 1897 the Managers had aimed to establish the new Boys' and Girls' schools 'on the same lines and of the same status as those at Hatcham'. Now they were more ambitious. In February 1909 the Governors decided to 'very materially raise the status of the Hampstead school'. The Charity Commissioners' Scheme dated 22 April 1910 contained a key detail: earlier ones had required the Charity's income to be equally divided between the four schools, but this allowed it to be divided 'as required', allowing the Governors to direct money to a particular school, by implication to Hampstead. The Scheme set the fees at £6 to £12 a year and allowed boys to remain until they were 19, enabling them to go direct to university.

A.J. Spilsbury, Headmaster, 1909.

Wagstaff responded to the 1906 reports and the Governors' policy of raising Haberdashers' status, giving it something of the academic quality he had found at Bradford and the character he had known at Oundle. He therefore cultivated specialist teaching, based form groups on science sets, took personal charge of science subjects, taught some science lessons, introduced setting to modern languages, and weeded out the few weak teachers. Early in 1910 he renamed the VI Form the Matriculation Form and expanded the Post-Matriculation Form as the new VI Form. He gave regular lectures to the Scientific Society, in 1916 joined it to the Literary and Debating Society as the School Society, and arranged visits to London factories, then a signal innovation. He impressed and pleased parents by holding open day exhibitions in addition to the already popular Commendation Days.

In March 1911 a report by the University of London found the curriculum 'well-suited to the requirements of the pupils', considered most of the staff 'well-qualified and highly efficient teachers, who succeed in inspiring the boys with their enthusiasm', and decided to 'congratulate the Governing Body on the recent extension of the premises and on their choice of a Headmaster. The Inspectors are much impressed by his administrative ability and open minded and sympathetic attitude, and believe that under his guidance the Haberdashers' Aske's School will become more and more valuable and efficient.'

The school was much inspected. In October 1911 the Board of Education's second report delivered a similar verdict, finding that 'There has been a satisfactory advance in the quality and standard of the work', noting that 'The assistant staff contains a good proportion of excellent teachers, who are well-qualified for the work they are doing', and stating that 'The Headmaster has high qualifications. The necessary reorganisation is being gradually and ably dealt with in his great task of making this School a thoroughly efficient Secondary School of the most advanced type.'

Wagstaff changed the school's character by modifying the House system, created by Percy Meadows, one of Hinton's new graduate teachers, a modest man with a dry sense of humour, and no mean cricketer – in 1907 he took 5 wickets for 26 runs in the Masters vs. 1st XI match. He used the Autumn Term 1903 *Skylark* to make a case for 'The House System in Athletics' in 'a good public school'. Such a school could be organised into four divisions called 'Houses' according to the initial letters of boys' surnames, each House with a name and a colour to be worn as a rosette on suitable occasions. Each House could elect its own captain and officers, hold meetings and organise its own affairs. It could discover and nurture sporting ability, encourage boys to play in representative games, raise standards and promote school spirit.

Meadows' ideas were popular and the House system was in place by the Summer Term of 1904. Each House had a captain and vice-captain in cricket and soccer, pledged to umpire and referee, and to select and coach teams. Haberdashers' was expected to place its teams 'first among North London Schools'. Only one problem emerged. Should the House names spell out the acronym 'ASKE' from their initial letters? It was soon solved: boys with surnames A to D became Crows House with blue as its colour; E to J Eagles, green; K to R, Magpies, red; S to Z Swifts, yellow.

However, during 1910 Wagstaff concluded that the avian names were rather contrived, and was suspicious of embryonic schoolboy democracy in the Houses, so argued that they needed the firm guidance of talented Housemasters. Thus by the end of the year he had reorganised the Houses on lines still recognisable today. Messrs. Calvert, Henderson, Jobling, Russell, Strouts and – naturally – Meadows were made Housemasters and gave their own names to the six new Houses. (Evidence of the change can be seen on the House Athletic, Cricket and Football shields, which are engraved with the 1906 and 1910 names.) Houses implied prefects. Hitherto the form

C.J.L. Wagstaff, Headmaster, 1910–19.

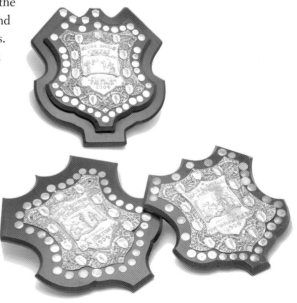

House shields, 1904. Cricket, (presented by the Freeman brothers), Athletics and Football.

Wagstaff with prefects, 1914.

captains had wielded authority amongst their fellow pupils, but in 1912 Wagstaff introduced prefects as a disciplinary force, and in 1913 arranged for the school to play an MCC team, so establishing an annual fixture that still exists.

John Gooch (Hampstead 1908–14) recorded his distant memories of the first Housemasters.

Calvert: 'Bung-eye', as he was known – either he'd got a glass eye or an eye which stared at you, nobody was ever quite sure which. He taught anything, and we used to do our damnedest, and pretty successfully too, to get him off the subject he was supposed to be teaching. Henderson taught English and History – he was a very clever man. At the thought of going up into his Form, I trembled. The idea didn't delight me at all. He was academically brilliant, but he should never have been a schoolmaster. I didn't think we'd get on at all together. Jobling was a marvellous fellow. Old Jobbo used to come to the Old Boys' Dinners, and they always used to get him a bit the worse for wear, and he used to reminisce. He was a very nice man and a wonderful swimmer. He'd got a broad pair of shoulders and I've seen him swimming down the school pool with a small boy sitting on his back and a sort of bow wave around him. Percy Meadows always wore a bow tie. He was an organist and a very good pianist. I remember listening to him during the Lord's Prayer in Morning Assembly, playing any number of variations on the usual tune. Russell was another musical man. He was a brilliant musician and taught English among other subjects. He was a bachelor and kept cats – mind you, this is hearsay, but these things get about with a modicum of truth. Strouts was a priceless old boy, really a very charming man. He had a very big tummy and was quite short. I've seen him sitting on the edge of a desk with his feet on the seat, which made him face the class, looking at some particular boy, with his cheeks puffed out, and the boy not knowing whether to laugh or cry, which I think used to amuse him.

The boys were extraordinarily enthusiastic. During 1903 cricket, football and swimming all flourished. An impressive series of activities and societies followed: in 1905 rifle shooting, in 1906 debating, in 1907 cadets, in 1910 golf and scouts, in 1911 Scientific and Dramatic Societies, and in 1914 the Gymnastic and Music Societies. Nor were the masters behind hand. Wagstaff's textbooks *Properties of Matter* and *Electricity* were rivalled by Russell's work as a composer (in 1895 he had taken a BMus at London University), and by history textbooks written by Messrs Calvert, Henderson and Meadows. It cannot be pretended that various masters' contributions to School Verse (1919) rise far above the level of doggerel, or that Henderson's numerous works on English language and literature, etc., are other than meritorious. However, his later autobiography, *Schoolmasters All*, revealed a waspish humour – much of it at the expense of his identifiable former colleagues.

Only the First World War checked this activity. Its origins lay partly in the imperialist fervour shown in the Boer War of 1899–1902. At least six OHs (E.W. Awberry, A.O. Buckingham, O. Green, E.S. Horton, W.D. Stenning and F.W. Wheeler) served in South Africa. In 1903 a representative of the War Office inspected the school's drill and reported that it was 'very elementary but promising'. During the 1904 Sports Day, the first to be held on the school's own field, the Master of the Haberdashers' Company, Mr Swayne

Dr Henderson's *Schoolmasters All*, 1933.

Cricket match at Hampstead, 1910.

TOP: Bugles bought for the cadets, 1914.

MIDDLE: Captain V. Reynolds, master, killed in action.

BOTTOM: Lieutenant E. Jobling, housemaster, mentioned in despatches.

Pearce, hoped 'that boys should qualify at school to defend the Empire in time of need'. Hinton reported to the parents that 'Shooting and Drill are encouraged by the War Office, the National Rifle Association and our own Governors', and that the school hoped to provide rifles and a miniature range.

By the end of the Autumn Term 1904 the school had a range and the Rifle Club was established in 1905, with 22 members coached by Strouts. Regular shooting matches began in 1906 when the school team competed in the Hampstead Patriotic Society's annual Empire Challenge Shield. By 1907 the club had 58 members and during the summer holiday 20 boys camped and shot at Bisley, led by three masters (the Revd Braine, Jobling and Strouts) and Sergeant Hartnett (late Colour Sergeant, 2nd Essex Infantry, school Instructor in PE).

In 1906 Haberdashers' Empire Day celebrations included 'a March Past' and a 'military salute to the flag', and in 1907 at the request of senior boys the school set up a Cadet Corps, commanded by the Revd Braine and equipped with a blue uniform with the school badge. However, the War Office refused to recognise it, so it was disbanded in November 1909 and succeeded by a Scout Troop. The Rifle Club flourished. During 1908 Commendation Day Hinton made a successful appeal for donations to buy match standard rifles. In 1910 the Shooting VIII came third in the Imperial Senior Challenge Shield (Empire Day) Competition, open to schools throughout the British Empire, and won the Frankfort Challenge Shield at Bisley.

The Corps was re-founded in October 1914, recognised by the London Territorial Force Association, and by July 1915 had 240 members and six officers led by Major Wagstaff and Captain Jobling. (Bugles bought in 1914 are displayed in the Cadet Corps Officers' Mess.) War Office funding was inadequate, so the school appealed to parents to buy rifles and equipment. By the end of the War 11 masters had served in the armed forces, including J.H. Blunt (wounded and captured on the Somme), Jobling (with the active service rank of Lieutenant, mentioned in despatches), and Capt. Reynolds (killed at Armentieres).

Skylark kept a melancholy record. F.J. Milne, former captain of the Rifle Club, in 1907 the school's best shot at Bisley, was the first OH fatality, on 14 November 1914 killed instantly near Le Touret when a shell burst over him whilst he was digging in shoulder to shoulder with his brother, who was fortunately unharmed. E.A.G. Coules was a brilliant pupil who won the school's Matriculation Prize in 1914, and passed third into Woolwich and second into the Royal Engineers in 1915, but on 28 October 1917 he was killed on the Somme and is buried at Roisel. A 2nd Lieutenant aged only 19, he is commemorated by the Coules Cup for marksmanship and by a beautifully engraved memorial plaque, maintained in pristine condition in the Cadet Corps quarters. It records his stoical final words: 'I'm all right; get on with the work.'

As masters left for the armed services (by March 1917 the school was short of five regular teachers) they were replaced by temporary masters and mistresses, not all of whom could keep order. Edward Mautner (1912–22, who endowed the Mautner Travel Grants and worked on the Stock Exchange until he was aged over 90) recalled that masters who had come out of retirement were disrespectfully dubbed 'dug outs' but that two of them were particularly popular, C.F. Venn and L.H. Edminson. Theodore McEvoy (1915–21, one of the first cadets accepted into Cranwell, later Sir Theodore) called them 're-treads' and recounted how

> Our licensed buffoon, F.H. Bedford, delighted to rag dear old Mr Edminson. In the wall of one form room there was a sliding panel through which Bedford, in the corridor, would poke his leering face to disrupt Edminson's German lesson. Edminson, eventually provoked beyond endurance, cried to us: 'After him! Catch him!' At which we all fled from the room and were not seen again for the rest of the lesson.

Over-influenced by the anti-German feeling of the day, the Governors told Wagstaff to list 'boys whose parents appeared to be legal subjects of the enemy'. By June 1915 he had identified two brothers named Scheiner, but advised that they were not a threat to the United Kingdom: the elder boy was about to follow his father to the USA and although the younger one was to stay in England with his Hungarian mother he was aged only 12. However, Wagstaff then began to puzzle over the allegiance of a boy named Goldner, whose father was Hungarian ('enemy') and mother Serbian ('friend'). In December 1915 the Governors resolved that Goldner's 'parents be requested to withdraw him' from the school. As if to balance this unfortunate chauvinism, the Governors offered places to the sons of Belgian refugees.

There were 230 old boy volunteers in the forces before the end of 1914, and 497 by the end of 1916, so the Roll of Honour quickly lengthened and the school started a fund for a memorial to the 107 dead almost as soon as the Armistice was declared. Nor did tragedy end then. Capt. H.A. Patey, DFC, caught Spanish flu on 14 February 1919 and died on the following Tuesday. Although aged only 15, in September 1914 he had joined the Royal

Second Lieutenant E.A.G. Coules, O.H., killed in action.

Coules Memorial.

In Memory of Eric A. G. Coules, 2ND Lt. R.E., Prize Cadet R.M.A. Woolwich, February 1916. Killed while commanding a working party in France, October 28TH 1917. Aged 19. May his last words to his men after being struck down be an inspiration to all here at his old school:— "I'm all right; get on with the work".

Captain H.A. Patey, D.F.C.

Naval Volunteer Reserve, from March to September 1916 fought at Gallipoli, in 1917 obtained a Commission in the Royal Naval Air Service, and in June 1918 received his decoration for a 'stunt'. He led his flight on a dawn raid behind the German lines, bombed an aerodrome, shot up the officers' quarters, attacked vehicles going up to the front, and then strafed trenches as he returned to base. However, the school learned that the conflict had not been all heroics when in the summer term of 1919 *Skylark* published Lt. K. McMillan's *My Life in the Army*, telling how his patriotic enthusiasm had been replaced by caution and war weariness. A memorial inscribed with the names of the 107 dead was unveiled in the assembly hall in 1922. When the school moved to Elstree it was placed in the then Chapel in Aldenham House.

The school itself had had a brief taste of war when on 19 October 1917 a Zeppelin dropped a bomb nearby, breaking 135 window panes. By early 1918 conscription had deprived the school of adequate domestic and maintenance staff, so the boys were organised into 'labour gangs' and Sir Theodore McEvoy recalled 'belonging to the window-cleaning gang and spending spare time on ladders with a chamois leather'. Normality was hardly restored when 'Waggie' Wagstaff (as he had come to be called by the boys) announced that he was soon to leave, and when in December 1919 he did leave to be Headmaster of King Edward VII School, King's Lynn, *Skylark* rightly judged that he had 'remodelled' Haberdashers'. He died in 1981 at the age of 106, remaining mentally active and alert to the last. A memorial plaque is displayed in the present Chapel, and the Wagstaff Memorial Prize is awarded at each Commendation Day.

At the end of the war, Haberdashers' faced a financial crisis. Since 1875 the Governors had struggled to find the sufficient income and capital for four schools. In 1910 they had concluded that the income from the aging Hoxton estate had peaked. During 1912 the Company had borrowed to begin modernisation at Hoxton, but repayments took most of the income from the new properties. The Governors also had to contend with staff salaries. In 1906 the LCC report had concluded that they were too low, and the Board of Education's report had stated: 'The salaries paid to the assistant teachers are very low, and quite unworthy of a secondary school.' In 1911 the Board's report had advised that higher salaries were necessary to recruit and retain highly qualified and experienced teachers.

Cadet Corps, 1914. C.J.L. Wagstaff, Headmaster, sitting third from left, other Officers and NCOs.

Staff at Hampstead, 1919. Back row from left: Mr Cushion, Mr Jones, Miss E.S. Challen, Mr Venn, Dr Henderson, Mr Adkins, Mr Calvert, Mr Jobling, Mr Ash, Mr Norton, Mr Gruner, Mr Hendry, Mr Webb, Miss G. Plante, Miss Barralet, Mr Strouts, Mr Paterson.
Front row: Miss C. Johnson, Mr George Blunt, Mr Edmonson, Mr Stokes, C.J.L.Wagstaff, Revd W.H. Braine, Mr John Blunt, Miss J.L. Biggs, Mr Meadows.

Wartime prices reduced the masters' standard of living, as they informed the Governors by letters and a deputation. In 1917 the Board of Education had issued a minimum scale of salaries and offered the Governors £3,600 to meet it, but it had not been enough. In 1920 they calculated that adopting salaries recommended by the Burnham Committee on Teachers' Remuneration would plunge their four schools into deficit, but in 1921 were obliged to pay Burnham rates of pay. Approached for help, Middlesex County Council offered a capitation grant of £10 for each of the 140 Hampstead pupils who lived within its own county boundary. Higher pay quickly helped the school to recruit new teachers, including 'Pop' Oliver, 'Bill' Crossman and 'Harry' Payne, each of whom stayed until well after the Second War.

In 1920 the Governors increased fees to 18 guineas a year and in 1921 raised them to 22 guineas. In 1911 the Board of Education report had noted that 44% of the school's pupils were too young to qualify for the £5 capitation grant. In 1921 the Preparatory Department was actually running at a loss. Thus the Governors closed it and used the space for older grant-attracting pupils. In 1926 the Board of Education proposed to end all capitation grants to endowed secondary schools if they also received similar financial assistance from local education authorities, although the LEA's were to continue to pay for free places. The Governors then accepted LCC grants for the two Hatcham schools but the Board's capitation grants, and Middlesex County Council's grants for capital expenditure, for Acton and Hampstead. The Board's grants accounted for about 25% of the school's income. In 1925 Middlesex County Council gave £4,000 of the £7,050 cost of new sports facilities and in 1928 provided £12,000 as a non-repayable loan covering virtually the whole cost of a new Science Building.

6

The Interwar Years
1920–1939

F.J. Kemp (later the Revd Kemp), an Oxford physicist, arrived from Clifton College in January 1920. The confidential annex to a 1921 Board of Education inspection, carried out when he had been at the school for little more than a year, described him presciently as 'suitable, unassuming but effective, and likely to attain his ends without friction'. A 1925 LCC report found him 'A man of unusual ability and of genial temperament who has clearly won the esteem and cooperation of his large staff', and recorded that he was introducing 'many important changes with the support of a keen and experienced governing body.'

His short-term aim was to gain Haberdashers' official public school status, and his long term one to continue Wagstaff's policy of improving its academic quality and giving it the atmosphere and character of a public school. The first aim was soon achieved. During 1922 Kemp was elected a member of the Headmasters' Conference, and he took the opportunity to change the school's main winter game from Association to Rugby football, which he coached with some skill. The second needed a little more time. However, when Russell, who had become Second Master on 'Puggy' Stokes' retirement in 1919, retired himself in 1926 little was left to link the school with its early days in Hoxton. (The Hatcham Boys' School had gained HMC status in 1913, but lost it in 1928 after becoming dependent on LCC grants.)

Kemp's first step to achieve his long-term aim was to carry out improvements recommended by the 1921 inspection report. The existing school library was a collection of reference books kept in a cupboard at the back of the assembly hall. In 1922 he added books on art, history, literature and science, and in 1925 opened an English fiction

The Operatic Society's first production, *HMS Pinafore*, 1934.

Cadet Corps Signal Platoon in the cellar at Chase Lodge, 1930.

section. By 1926 he had increased the total stock to over 2,000 volumes, housed in a room converted from the former pavilion, part of which he also equipped as an armoury and orderly room for the Cadet Corps. (The 1925 report noted that 'The Cadet Corps is strong in numbers [14 officers and 427 other ranks] and the efficiency and tone reflect great credit on the commanding and other officers.') He found space for a prefects' room and a junior laboratory, installed heating in the gymnasium, equipped dedicated history and geography rooms, and the Governors provided more laboratories by constructing the Science Building, opened by the Duke of Connaught, now generally known as Prince Arthur, in 1931. The ornate key that he used is preserved in the school archives.

His second step was to strengthen the House system. He ensured that boys sat at House tables in the Dining Hall, instituted the Work and Conduct trophy, and put the Cadets on a House basis. By 1925 there were 15 House trophies and Meadows won nine of them. The Meadows House Captain claimed 'We are now "officially" the crack House of the school. This is all that a House can wish for. The Summer Holidays brought to a close the most successful year that any House ever had.'

His third step was to promote sport. Before the First World War cricket and football had been voluntary, but he made games compulsory, introduced boxing in 1921, water-polo in 1925, and fives in 1930, and in the words of the 1925 report appointed two 'very enthusiastic' PE teachers who 'were working very hard to inculcate the spirit of team work' and fostering 'a splendid spirit' amongst the boys. In 1925 he persuaded the Governors to provide extra playing fields for cricket and rugby by buying Chase Lodge and its grounds in Mill Hill, and to add further land in 1926.

His fourth step was to encourage extra curricular activities. He allowed a period a week to school societies, supported the Dramatic Society's spring term productions, and facilitated expeditions and trips in the summer term. In 1927 'Harry' Payne, an ex-officer and all-round sportsman who had faced dismissal for falsely claiming that he was a Cambridge

BELOW LEFT: Prince Arthur opening the Science Building, 1931.

RIGHT: The new Science Building.

THE HABERDASHERS' ASKE'S HAMPSTEAD SCHOOL
OPERATIC SOCIETY

presents

THE
MIKADO

(by permission of R. D'Oyly Carte, Esq.)

by

W. S. GILBERT and ARTHUR SULLIVAN

on

January 16th, 17th and 18th, 1936

HABERDASHERS' ASKE'S HAMPSTEAD SCHOOL
DRAMATIC SOCIETY

presents

MACBETH

by

WILLIAM SHAKESPEARE

Thursday, Friday and Saturday,
20th, 21st and 22nd January, 1938

TOP: *The Mikado*, 1936; ABOVE: *Macbeth*, 1938.

graduate, redeemed himself by organising an exhibition on the relationship between education and employment in industry. 1933 was a busy year. The science and geography departments held open evenings, when parents were entertained with light refreshments. Percy Meadows, a skilled pianist, formed the Operatic Society, which specialised in performing Gilbert and Sullivan. The Dramatic Society produced its first full-length Shakespeare play, *Henry IV Part I*, followed in 1938 by *Macbeth*. In 1934 a party of boys and masters made the school's first foreign tour, to Germany. In 1937 the Old

Haberdashers' Rugby Football Club officially opened its sports ground and pavilion at Croxdale Road in Boreham Wood, now headquarters of the Old Haberdashers' Association.

His fifth step was to introduce school uniform. There was no uniform in the first 20 years at Hampstead. Junior boys dressed in multi-coloured blazers, tweed jackets, or woollen jumpers. Senior boys wore suits or Norfolk jackets. By 1913 each new boy was issued with a cap to which was sewn a house button, and a metal lapel badge (similar to the present prefects' badges). Sixth form caps had a white band around the back. In 1924 Kemp introduced the still-existing uniform of dark blue blazer with crested badge and blue and white tie for most boys, and the long-forgotten black jackets with pin-striped trousers for sixth formers and prefects. In school, prefects wore a black velvet cap with a gold tassel, and recipients of rugby colours a similar blue cap with a silver tassel. Out of school, prefects and members of senior teams playing away matches wore bowler hats, in the summer replaced by boaters, complementing the prefects' seasonal scarlet blazers.

Kemp's sixth step, but by no means his least, was to review examinations and teaching. On moving to Hampstead Haberdashers' had concentrated on Cambridge Locals and London Matriculation, but in 1908 the Governors had affiliated their four schools to London University and thus the school switched to the London exams, entering boys for Senior and Junior Matriculation, in 1917 replaced by the School Certificate and Higher School Certificate. Kemp found that almost all work in the small sixth form (in 1921 only 28 boys were aged over 16) was in mathematics and science, so he decided to expand the sixth and diversify teaching by consolidating a popular commercial course and promoting 'the Arts side', whilst directing the boys' parents' attention to Oxford and Cambridge as suitable universities.

His achievement was recognised in the Board of Education's 1932 inspection report. 'The Head Master is well fitted for his post by academic attainment and teaching experi-

F.J. Kemp, Headmaster, 1920–1940.

Dramatic Society production of *The Ghost Train*, 1932.

Boys setting off on one of the first School trips abroad, 1930s.

School Entrance Exam, General Knowledge Paper, 1922.

ence, and by the personal qualities of tact and judgement which make for the successful conduct of a large school.' The report added 'The staff is adequate numerically and well qualified academically, as a whole maintains a sound level of teaching and contains a good proportion of men of first rate ability. The excellent organisation of the corporate activities affords evidence of keenness and devotion.'

The report commented: 'The most striking change within the last ten years has been the development of Sixth Form work.' The number of sixth formers had risen to 77, and the number taking 'Arts' subjects had increased from virtually nil to 31. Thus most boys who left the sixth form still joined business, commerce and the professions, but the school had 'maintained and strengthened its links with the Universities' and in the last three years 33 boys had entered a university, eight after winning entrance scholarships (plus two scholarships to medical school).

The report was distinctly positive. The 'fine Science block' had made 'very adequate provision' for all aspects of the subject. Kemp had recently allowed 'abler boys' to take the School Certificate exam in four years instead of five and work reached a 'good standard' in biology, English, geography and mathematics, which was being reorganised by the newly-designated head of department, 'Pop' Oliver, 'a first-rate teacher', who was soon responsible for a series of scholarships to his old Cambridge College, Jesus. Sixth-form work in mathematics, science and modern studies was of 'good quality' and in the last three years 52 boys had won Higher School Certificates, including 29 distinctions.

The Lower School, efficiently and enthusiastically supervised by its own Head, J.H. Blunt (nicknamed 'Josh'), ably assisted by Miss Constance Johnson (almost inevitably known as 'Connie'), 'an exceptionally good teacher of young boys', was a distinct disciplinary and pastoral unit with its own facilities housed in a separate wing of the building, where boys were taught for two years by masters from the Senior School before

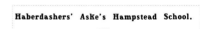

Haberdashers' Aske's Hampstead School.
—
GENERAL KNOWLEDGE PAPER.
WEDNESDAY, 13th SEPTEMBER, 1922.

1. In a recent newspaper the following were mentioned. Write *one* sentence about each. (a) Irregulars. (b) The Falling Mark. (c) Sunday Games. (d) If Winter Comes. (e) Key Industries. (f) Genoa. (g) The Dalton Plan. (h) Soviet. (i) Impressionist. (j) Honours List. (k) Cathal Bruga. (l) Stymie. (m) Centre Court. (n) Court of Appeal. (o) Washington Treaties. (p) All out for 15. (q) Reparations. (r) Chukker. (s) Autumn Session. (t) Proportional Representation.

2. With what holiday resorts are the following associated: (a) A Wheel and a Tower. (b) Volk. (c) The Brig. (d) The Leas. (e) Pirates. (f) Dove Cottage. (g) A return tourist fare of 41/-. (h) Sir George Newnes. (i) Fairlight Glen. (j) Sir Dan Godfrey.

3. Give a list of ten articles of food and drink which are subject to Customs or Excise Duties, and state the amount of the Duty.

4. In what famous pictures do the following appear? Name also the Artists and approximate dates. (a) A boy drinking from a stream. (b) A harp with one string. (c) Two little boys with wings (at the foot of the picture). (d) Two men sawing a log. (e) A King holding a sword horizontally behind his head.

5. Give the titles, composers, and one or two details, of the works from which the following quotations are made:—

(a) (b)

(c) (d)

(e)

P.M.

Staff at Hampstead, 1920s. Back row, left to right: Miss G.M. King, Miss J.L. Biggs, Miss E.S. Challen, Miss C. Johnson. Middle row, left to right: Mr Gruner, Dr Abson, Mr Crossman, Mr Oliver, Mr Payne, Mr Adkins, Mr J. Blunt, Mr Venn, Mr Webb, Mr Paterson, Mr Calvert, Mr Sturgeon, Mr Gibbs, Mr Small, Mr Rawnsley. Front row, left to right: Mr Ash, Mr Meadows, Mr Strouts, Mr Russell, Rev F.J. Kemp (Headmaster), Dr Henderson, Rev W.H. Braine, Mr Edmonson, Mr Norton.

School Swimming Team, 1934.

transferring there, usually aged 12. The report's main criticism of the curriculum in the Senior School was that music was taught only to junior boys, but the Governors refused to have it taught more widely: the Deputy Chairman, Mr Carr, told the inspectors that 'it was a waste of money teaching music to non-musical people, he had wasted a lot on his own family'.

The 1911, 1921 and 1932 reports show to what extent the school had changed in simple statistical terms. It had grown from 535 to 554 to 602 boys, and from 27 to 28 to 32 teachers. From 1921 to 1932 the proportion of boys from Middlesex had increased from 55% to 75%. The proportion of boys receiving free places had risen from 12.5% to 16% to 17%, but the proportion from working-class backgrounds had remained remarkably stable at 4%, 5% and 6%, indicating a middle-class clientele.

The school's atmosphere in the 1920s and 1930s is easy to recapture. It was adopting a character longer-established public schools were questioning. A *Skylark* article on 'The Public School Spirit' declared, 'To wear a double-breasted waist coat may do no harm to oneself; it certainly harms the reputation of the school'. In contrast to the policy adopted in 1875, Kemp regarded corporal punishment as the norm, so allowed masters and prefects to beat boys. Sitting either side of Kemp, the prefects stare out from their annual photograph, grim-faced and square-jawed, quite prepared to cane boys, as parents occasionally complained. Beneath the respectable surface there was some illicit activity. Bullying was quite common and there was sporadic smoking (a caning offence), although apparently very little obscenity or swearing. However, Eric Treacy, later Bishop of Wakefield, who joined the school in 1918, recalled that a coy young woman used to haunt the school gates in the afternoon and was the object of a good deal of adolescent boasting and suggestiveness.

Treacy considered the standard of teaching pretty low, that the school had no great influences or influencers, and that Kemp was dull and joyless. He felt one master was too fond of cuddling the boys and another too fond of caning them, and thought his best friend amongst the adults was the groundsman. Although not an academic success, Treacy was a noted sportsman; twice Heavyweight Boxing and Shot champion, member of the First XV, Captain of Russells Cricket and Head of the House itself. A Sergeant in the Corps, his school reports on 'Character' referred to his 'powers of leadership', perhaps not entirely mistakenly. Indeed, it is possible that the article on 'Cricket Games' which he wrote for *Skylark* in 1924, arguing that the sport's 'noble influence in life' was to teach boys the spirit of fair play in a wider sense owed something to the school's own values. The school certainly thought highly enough of him to remit half his fees during his final year, 1924/25.

Most Old Haberdashers (OHs) of that time recall the school with affection, as did Ken Blessley, who joined the school in April 1920, aged six. He told that almost all boys walked to school, in the morning encouraged by the five-to-nine bell, which rang from a turret high on the roof. The day began with registration and a brief service in the assembly hall. Some boys returned home for lunch, but many paid 1/- a day for a school dinner, served in two sittings in the dining hall, where the prefects had a separate table and the masters sat on a raised dais, both groups benefiting from a wider choice of food. Everyday discipline was strict, maintained by prefects who included some over-enthusiastic beaters. Masters intervened only in serious cases; for example, when nobody owned up after a snowball containing a stone hit 'Bill' Crossman, Kemp asked each of the six housemasters to cane the 50 or so senior boys in his House.

Sport played an important part in the school's life, but the Cadet Corps was perhaps more prominent, its status guaranteed by the First War: 11 a.m. on 11 November was observed with a service in the assembly hall, ended by the Last Post and Reveille sounded

The Duke of York's Camp, 1923.

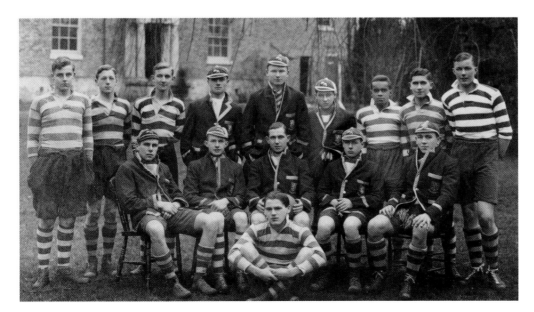

First XV at Chase Lodge, 1930.

by the Corps buglers in the gallery. Outside, all trains stopped for two minutes on the main line to St Pancras station. Membership of the Corps was obligatory from the age of 11, so some 400 boys were divided into five infantry companies, a signals section and a band. Attached to the Royal Fusiliers, the Corps practised drill with Lee Enfield rifles on one afternoon a week, and on the annual field day the band led a column of boys kitted out in peaked service caps, buttoned tunics and puttees, as they marched to Hampstead Heath or to Brondesbury Station to travel to Richmond Park. The Labour government abolished the Corps in 1930, but the annual summer camp survived, and was complemented by attendance at the Duke of York's much-publicised camps for 'industrial' and 'public school' boys.

Gordon Wallwork (1931–40) confirmed that until the outbreak of war the school remained much as Ken Blessley described it, the good out-of-class discipline being sustained by sixth formers who enjoyed 'Sixth Form Powers and Privileges' (being excused roll call for assembly, giving lines, using the main entrance, but wearing the white-banded cap). Ken Blessley looked 'back on the teaching staff as decent people with sensible attitudes' and singled out 'three exceptional men', Abson (who taught French), 'Stookie' Sturgeon (a talented cricketer) and Youd (a fine rugby coach). Gordon Wallwork stressed that the strict classroom discipline was intended to produce the best

Inter-house cross country race through Hampstead, 1925.

possible School Certificate results, and that only a minority of masters used the cane to keep order. He concluded that 'there were a number of excellent masters, the standard of teaching was generally high'. David Godrich (1939-45) agreed: 'one of the most memorable aspects of school life was the esprit de corps we all felt for the institution and in particular the masters. No master made any boy more important than another, demonstrating the high standard of fairness that prevailed at all times'.

Professor Andrew Booth (1930–37) recalled several teachers with respect, and Mr Rawnsley in particular:

SPEISEKARTE·

The front of the programme for *Speisekarte*, 1936.

> In the sixth form I had Lee Rawnsley who was another splendid teacher as well as being a real 'character'. He used to drive up to the school in a yellow sports car and skid to a halt. In 1936 he wrote and produced a musical review *Speisekarte*, based on the then smash hit *White Horse Inn* playing at the London Coliseum. Rawnsley's physics was completely up to date and included exposure to the new quantum mechanics and to elementary relativity. He had many unusual experiments for those interested. These included spectroscopy and the diffusion of metallic sodium through glass. When I started teaching as a university lecturer in 1945 I was able to use Rawnsley's notes for my first year physics.

Kenneth Jermy (1932–39) long-remembered 'the unforgettable "Doughie" Rawnsley. He was the only master who taught "examination technique" and he also advised us to stop swotting a week before any important exam: "If you don't know it by then, you never will."' Rawnsley had lost a leg serving with the Royal Flying Corps in the First War, but was recalled at the start of the Second, stationed with the Balloon Barrage HQ and Air Staff at Bentley Priory in Stanmore, and promoted to Squadron Leader and Wing Commander before his release in 1944, after which he farmed in Devon.

David Jones (1927–34) remembered many of the masters of the day. A.C.F. Beales who taught him History later became a prolific academic author and Professor at King's College, London. 'Pop' Oliver taught Maths with a 'delightful Scottish brogue'; Percy Meadows played the grand piano in assembly (the Hall gained an organ only in 1936); 'Bill' Crossman was 'an outgoing character with a sharp voice'; Youd was 'a stout, robust Yorkshireman'; Calvert 'always wore a mortar board alone, without a gown'; Sturgeon, 'tall and red-headed was very keen, and disliked draughty classrooms, so it was very funny when his lessons followed those by 'Porky' Pask, who was very much a fresh air man – with open windows that had suddenly to be slammed shut'. Pask himself was 'a very robust gent who had a sense of humour'.

'Chaucer' Henderson was well-known for his grammar textbook, *The English Way*; Paterson 'always went about hatless and with a walking stick'; Fluke, 'a tough character from Liverpool, enjoyed taking part in Gilbert and Sullivan and playing Rugger'; Adkins insisted that boys entered his classroom 'marching in twos, to the beat of his swagger stick'; Gruner 'believed in the psychological approach and beat no one'; 'Wally' Ash was 'a Welsh character with a booming voice whose favourite remark after misbehaviour was "Give me your diary, boy" so that he could enter a demerit'; the Revd Braine was 'very small with a red face, and it was rumoured that he had been a rowing cox at Cambridge, and at a party had pretended to be a ventriloquist's doll'; and 'Nobby' Norton was 'a

Mr Lee Rawnsley.

School Scout Camp, 1936.

robust teacher who believed in very moderate corporal punishment, and once threatened to use a bat to beat a whole junior cricket team, but was very popular' receiving letters from OHs all over the world.

'Josh' Blunt was another 'formidable character and a respected and very kind man'; Webb appeared 'an elderly gent who was very near retirement'; Abbot seemed 'in frail health, but was splendid at Cadet Camp concert parties'; 'Uncle Jeff' Cooper always 'did a prodigious amount of writing on the board'; Hurrell was 'a very tall and kindly master who on Friday afternoons held his classes spellbound with Sherlock Holmes stories'; and Rawnsley was 'a very broad spoken Yorkshireman'; whilst Hedley, 'an excellent games coach', left to become Head of PT at Mill Hill School, and eventually Lt. Colonel in charge of PT at GHQ Cairo; Mr Griffiths, 'a good teacher and very likeable man' unfortunately ultimately died of the after-effects of being gassed in the First War.

Despite the First World War's lasting influence, and the presence of so many veterans amongst the teachers, when touring Germany in 1934 the boys did not appreciate that their own vivid experiences foreshadowed the Second World War. They found it 'amusing' when German customs officials confiscated the Sunday Express at the border and thought it 'good fortune to be present at the parades' in Nuremberg. When in 1936 John Dudderidge, who had joined the staff in 1931, was a member of the British canoe team at the Olympics in Berlin, his Quaker background and pacifist convictions made him more observant. He noted that although foreign teams were cheered through the streets, the canoeists were quartered in 'a large modern police barracks' isolated from the Olympic Village and Stadium, were prevented from visiting any other events until the canoeing was over, and that many of the officials were soldiers.

Others were even more observant. When Prince Arthur re-visited Haberdashers' in 1936 he called upon the boys to be ready to defend the Empire. The Coronation of King George VI and Queen Elizabeth in May 1937 was an ideal opportunity to promote patriotism. Two members of the Corps joined a detachment of the British National Cadet Association for a parade on Constitution Hill and marched in the Royal Procession. Three cadets were invited to an Empire Service of Youth in Westminster Abbey and mused that the Tomb of the Unknown Warrior 'looked more wonderful than ever'. Boys who attended the Empire Rally of Youth in the Royal Albert Hall heard Stanley Baldwin make his last major speech as Prime Minister, declaiming that he handed the burden of duty to them, the sons of the British Empire, before proceedings ended with Jerusalem.

Thomas Elliott (1930–37) recalled that after the government disbanded the Cadet Corps in 1930, 'Dickie' Small kept the Signal Platoon going in mufti as the Signal Society, which held its own annual camps. In 1935 the Rifle Club was revived and in September 1936 the War Office re-established the Corps, in 1937 giving it OTC status and attaching it to the Brigade of Guards with retired RSM Wynes as the permanent instructor. Kenneth Jermy remembered that 'Wynes had a hut and an armoury on the school field, and we loved to call in during the lunch break, to hear his yarns about the regular army.' The governors responded with £125 for a new rifle range, followed in 1939 with £30 to allow the school shooting VIII to resume its attendance at Bisley. Training was a serious business: 'One of our star cadets was A.J. Mulligan, who became a Squadron Leader in the RAF.'

Officer Training Corps in the Assembly Hall, 1939.

Many sixth formers were confused about political issues. Some new young masters treated the boys as individuals with minds of their own, introducing them to radical authors such as Auden and Lawrence, and inducing the more intellectual ones to adopt their own left wing views. John Bambrough (1931–38, who left school to read English at New College, Oxford, and after the war was appointed Dean of Wadham and President of Linacre) wrote that his generation expected London and all major cities to be flattened by bombs and the whole country carpeted with poison gas.

We were convinced at one and the same time of the need to 'Fight Fascism' and of the wrongness of war and re-armament. This was the familiar dilemma of the Left Wing at that period; I think we vaguely felt that the answer lay in some form of passive resistance.

Thus some sixth formers objected to the re-establishment of the Corps and those already in the sixth were allowed to opt out.

7

The Impact of War

1939–1946

During the Munich Crisis of 1938 the Home Office, LCC and Middlesex County Council drew up an Air Raid Evacuation Scheme and drafted plans for the school to go to Monmouth, St Albans or Bedford. However, Kemp canvassed the views of existing and of prospective parents and decided that the school would stay in London, but arrange to evacuate any boys whose parents wished them to leave, a decision apparently backed by most of the parents and senior members of the teaching staff.

But when the War began on 3 September 1939 some parents arranged to send their sons to safety out of London. Twenty were evacuated to Wellingborough, and few of the expected new boys turned up, so numbers in the school fell from over 500 to fewer than 400. The start of term was delayed because the Auxiliary Fire Service took over the school, except for the Science Building, which became the Sixth Form quarters, where 'Harry' Payne, now the Senior Science Master, organised the Fire Watch. Most boys moved to Chase Lodge, where the house, changing rooms and pavilion were hastily turned into crowded and inadequate classrooms. The winter of 1939/40 was the third worst of the century (outdone only by the near arctic conditions of early 1947 and 1963) and the site soon revealed its disadvantages: coal fires struggled to resist the icy, snow-bearing winds, and there were no cooking facilities to provide hot meals. The petrol shortage and blackout made it difficult and dangerous to travel, so many boys left their homes to stay with friends and relatives in Mill Hill.

Inevitably, the normal school routine was disrupted. Few boys received more than three and a half days of teaching a week.

Bomb damage in Hampstead.

Chase Lodge, 1940.

Compulsory games were abandoned, House and school matches were rare events, the school play was cancelled, and most societies ceased to meet. The situation was eased a little in January 1940 when the Junior School was allowed to have afternoon lessons in part of Copthall County Girls' High School nearby. In August 1940 the school regained the use of most of the Hampstead site and the Junior School moved back from Chase Lodge. The Modern Sixth stayed at Chase Lodge, whilst the Fifths and Fourths alternated between there and Hampstead, a complex and time-consuming arrangement intended to give them access to science laboratories and to keep both sites occupied in order to deter another takeover. The Governors considered returning the whole school to Hampstead, but the Battle of Britain changed their minds. They also wisely cancelled a service in St Paul's Cathedral planned for Saturday 28 September 1940, intended to mark the 250th anniversary of the 1690 Act of Parliament.

Kemp had coped manfully with the problems caused by the outbreak of war, but had become seriously ill, so was absent for the second half of the Autumn Term in 1939, leaving the school in the care of Dr P.A. Abson, Second Master since 1931. Kemp returned during 1940 but had a relapse and delegated many of his duties to Abson before resigning in December, when the Governors appointed Abson to take his place. Kemp died of cancer on 27 December 1943, consumed by anxiety for his wife who was desperately ill in a nursing home in distant Torquay. Although some boys had regarded him as aloof and remote, he was in fact a shy and reserved man who shunned publicity and did good by stealth, particularly by private advice and encouragement. *Skylark* recorded that 'No school function lacked his presence and that of Mrs Kemp. The school was his major interest in life' and rightly considered that although Wagstaff had left 'what could become a great school' Kemp's 'energy and enterprise' had raised it to an unprecedented level of 'prosperity and repute'. (Appropriately, the Kemp Memorial Prize and Library were established in his memory, and for many years the latter was a separate section of the school library.)

Abson had a more commanding and outgoing personality. Educated at London University, he had taught Modern Languages at Haberdashers' since 1921. A fine scholar, with the gift of arousing enthusiasm for language and literature, and a genuine and sympathetic interest in his pupils, he had been form master to the Modern Sixth and had earned his reputation as an effective teacher by guiding 5R (fifth form repeaters) through School Certificate French. His brief was to hold the school together during the war – no easy task. He led by example. Although over the age limit, he volunteered for the Fire Watch and insisted on taking the unpopular Saturday night shift. He was on duty during the night of 10–11 May 1941, the occasion of London's worst air raid of the war.

Many boys enjoyed the Fire Watch. Dennis L. Cooper-Jones (1937–42) recalls that the team of masters and boys on duty was based in the Staff Common Room, but that on quiet and fine summer nights the boys slept out on the field and at dawn woke covered in dew, unless they had been disturbed earlier by P.A.H. Wyatt, a brilliant pianist, playing Chopin by moonlight shafting into the School Hall. Sidney Holt (1937–43) remembers:

> When we had to be inside at night a pastime of one group of us fire watchers was playing jazz in the assembly hall because the only available keyboard was the school organ. One evening the then Headmaster, Kemp, decided to pay a visit to see how all his brave lads were doing – I can still see his amazed and then darkening face. After that, although there was no absolute ban on jazz on the school premises, the hall and its organ were severely out of bounds.

Dr P.A. Abson, Headmaster 1940–45.

Some sixth formers then decided to entertain themselves by other means. David Godrich testifies: 'Fire watching developed into a social crisis when "Harry" Payne discovered that certain girls had been invited to "assist" in the night's activities!'

At the end of the Spring Term 1942 *Skylark* claimed that although short staffed (eight masters had left for the armed services in the first year of the war, and ten eventually did so) the school had 'returned as far as possible to its pre-war normality'. In reality, the school was profoundly changed. As Cooper-Jones says, 'The old way of life had disappeared for ever.' During 1940 the annual summer camp was replaced by what became an annual harvest camp, and a party of boys and masters was issued with passes to enter the South East Security Zone to work on a farm near Mereworth in Kent, toiling with horse-drawn machinery to alleviate the nation's food shortage. In October 1940 the OTC was transformed into the Junior Training Corps, and in January 1941 the Air Training Corps was set up.

Some boys became politically conscious. During 1940 an article in *Skylark* attacked 'irresponsible plutocracy' and advocated redistributive taxation to provide equal educational opportunities for all. At Easter 1943 several sixth formers attended an inter-school course on world affairs organised by the Ministry of Information. *Skylark* reported that although a talk by Konni Zilliacus (in 1949 expelled from the Parliamentary Labour Party for being pro-Communist) 'did not meet with universal agreement', a large majority of those discussing Russia 'voted the Russian system of government the best yet tried'.

The old boys also changed. The occasionally rather affected letters sent to *Skylark* by undergraduates at Oxford and Cambridge ('Jeremy wields a pretty hose in the Jesus Fire

Second World War Memorial at Elstree.

A VI flying over London.

Brigade') were soon replaced by letters written by men on active service. They made light of danger by adopting a highly nonchalant style and tone. In 1942 Sgt. H.G. Newstead described the Nazi attack on Greece and apologised for 'what my pals would call an awful "line shoot"'. L. Cpl. W.R. ('Nobbly') Tanner, a stalwart of the OH, dismissed his time as a prisoner of war in North Africa as 'an interesting and vaguely exciting yarn'. Capt. J.W. Hammond testified from Libya that 'Dr Abson built better than he may have thought: the Free French understood my French.'

During 1943 the school did seem to settle down. There was an impressive number of House and school matches. The Music Society was founded, followed in 1944 by the Philatelic and Archaeological Societies, and by the revival of the Chess Society. Abson increased the School Library's stock to 4,280 volumes, and *Skylark* became a little more detailed and expansive, publishing Brian Sewell's poem 'Faces in the Fire', whose title closely echoes a poem by John Ruskin, the nineteenth-century art critic, polemicist and social commentator.

Once again, appearances were deceptive. Abson was struggling to ensure Haberdashers' survival. 'Josh' Blunt, who had taught at the school since 1905, retired in December 1942, and was commemorated by the Blunt Memorial Prize. In April 1943 he was followed by 'J.B.' Paterson, Head of Science since 1906, the school's last link with the days before the First War. Parents were tempted to withdraw their sons at 15 or 16 to allow them to do vital and well-paid war work. Revised call-up regulations issued by the Ministry of Labour and National Service in 1942 made it almost impossible for sixth formers to study arts subjects at university unless they were sponsored by the armed forces. In March 1943 the Air Ministry actually began to recruit into the RAF directly from the school's Air Training Corps, a policy that threatened to reduce the number of sixth form pupils.

In October 1940 a delayed-action bomb had badly damaged the school. During 1944 peril returned. The Summer Term was dubbed 'doodle bug' term after the nickname given to the V1s (often called rockets, but technically jet-powered pilot-less planes, or flying bombs). Some parents kept their sons at home or sent them out of London, as in 1939, and those who did attend school often ran for the trenches and shelters several times a day, abandoning lessons to do so. Lunch was served in relays, in case a V1 hit the crowded dining hall, or a large number of meals spoiled on the tables after masters and boys alike had taken cover. The senior boys played a large part in holding the school together. 'Harry' Payne, also master-in-charge of cricket, wrote:

> There was an inescapable feeling of pride in British youth to see the final of the House cricket matches being imperturbably played at Chase Lodge, while V1s streamed steadily over NW London, with the injunction 'straight to the trenches' if the watchful master's whistle should blow.

A VI propanganda leaflet dropped by German planes.

The school's own exams were cancelled, but the School Certificate exams continued in those trying conditions.

In October 1940 a master, W.T. Whewell, captain of the Corinthian Casuals, and his wife were killed when a bomb destroyed their house. Later in the month a boy, M.G. Gluss, was killed in an air raid, and in February 1944 a recent leaver, J. Hepburn, lost his life in a V1 attack. Eighty-seven OHs made the ultimate sacrifice in the War, as did a master, Major M.R.G. Watkin, a member of the Intelligence Corps who fell in Austria in May 1945, a few days before the conflict ended. Kenneth Jermy believed that 'A particular loss was Denis Mann, a true all-rounder: School Captain, Scholar of Jesus College, Cambridge, and a master of every sport devised; a socialist, he registered as a conscientious objector and died while serving with an Ambulance Unit of the Society of Friends.' (A Book of Remembrance given by the OHA in 1948 is in a glass case at the foot of the First World War memorial in Aldenham House. An inscribed stone memorial, originally sited in a Garden of Remembrance at Chase Lodge, is outside the House in the grounds, overlooking the Croquet Lawn.)

An OH writes about the war.

However, some OHs had what was called a 'good war'. Derek Bond(1933–36), in 1984 president of Equity, the actors' trade union, won the MC with the Grenadier Guards, and wrote up his experiences in *Steady, Old Man! Don't You Know There's a War On?* (1990). Alan Whicker, the well-known broadcaster, recalled in Whicker's War (2005) that his time in the Corps helped him to gain a Commission that eventually led him to command the Army Film Unit in Italy and to accept the surrender of the SS headquarters in Milan. Ashe Lincoln (1922–24), the distinguished lawyer, who died in 1998 aged 90, recounted his early years in the war in his Secret Naval Investigator (1961). After volunteering for the Commandos he was twice mentioned in dispatches and was one of the first British officers to cross the Remagen bridge, the only one over the Rhine left standing by the retreating German army.

The most decorated OH was Albert Dreyfus (1929–32), who served with the French Army from 1939 to 1940, then made his way to England and joined the Free French under

Alan Whicker, OH, took charge of the Army Film Unit in Italy during the war.

De Gaulle and Le Clerc, receiving not only the Legion d'Honneur (Chevalier), but the Medaille Militaire and the Croix de Guerre. After Dunkirk his brother Manuel (1928–35) fought with the Free French Forces of the Interior as an underground resistance leader, known in the Limoges region by his nom de guerre of Commandant Marcel. They were both awarded the US Army Citation.

For several decades the demands of national security made it impossible for Professor I.J. Good (1928–35) to reveal that he had been engaged on crucial top-secret work (the 'Ultra' secret) alongside the most brilliant men of his generation, decoding German wireless messages at Bletchley Park in Buckinghamshire. With a personality 'not that of an officer and a gentleman, rather that of a philosopher and mathematician', he was not expected to join the army and was recruited for Bletchley via his top-level contacts in British chess. One of Good's bosses there was the now legendary Alan Turing, and Good regarded himself as his 'main statistical assistant', remarking laconically that his 'logical thinking was profound, but it wasn't fast'.

At the end of 1944 Abson had informed the Governors that he had decided to retire in June 1945, but they persuaded him to reconsider. However, he was knocked down by a taxi and badly concussed on the evening of 13 April 1945, and after spending some time in hospital he resigned with effect from the end of June. The Governors asked 'Pop' Oliver, in January 1941 Abson's choice as Second Master, to take charge temporarily as acting head until they had chosen and appointed a new Headmaster. Oliver paid Abson a generous tribute: 'From the first, the good of the school was his only concern, and so it has been to the very end of his career.' When Abson died unexpectedly on 22 September 1952 *Skylark* justly noted that 'P.A.' as he was affectionately known 'was liked and respected by all who knew him'. Abson's framed photograph is displayed in the Old Refectory in Aldenham House, and his name is perpetuated in the Abson Memorial Prize for Modern Languages.

Whoever the Governors appointed as the new Headmaster would face a difficult situation. Emeritus Professor John Holmes (1941–49) recalls that the boys had endured increasing strain. Throughout the war school dinners were unappetising; meat undercooked, gristly, stringy, tough and flavourless, vegetables bland and watery, puddings stolid, and fresh fruit and salads almost wholly absent. The Tuck Shop provided welcome supplements, including sticky, penny buns and doughnuts. Early in the war, the school had only taken to the shelters when raiders were reported 'imminent' but when the V1s appeared their swift flight and random destination made it necessary to spend more time in the cold and uncomfortable shelters, carefully listening for the sound of their engines rising in volume as they approached the school, then falling as they passed by. The V2s (genuine rockets) were less easy to endure. Travelling at supersonic speeds, they gave no warning, and their approach noise came after the devastating explosion. At least the listeners knew that they had survived. Nor did they have any doubt that Britain would win.

Like most people, the boys wanted an early end to wartime conditions, but were disappointed as food rationing continued and the damaged Hampstead site was but slowly repaired. Some thought discipline to be arbitary and poorly handled, 'diary marks' (which could lead to a detention or caning) seemingly given out according to a master's or a prefect's mood not according to the magnitude of the supposed offence, and minor matters (such as not wearing a school cap in the street) receiving undue prominence. On the other hand, there was some bullying and fist-fights were not uncommon, so a modicum of control was needed.

'Pop' Oliver's interregnum between Abson and the new Headmaster proved a precarious time for discipline as senior boys resented the imposition of peacetime routine. However Oliver, an ex-naval officer who had fought at Jutland in 1916, was a formidable character and not until after he had stepped down did a bottle of gin make a brief appearance in the prefects' room during a sixth form dance and his successor's car mysteriously find its way to the top of the coke heap near the entrance to the school boiler room. Oliver is remembered with the H.C. Oliver Prize for Service to the Senior School.

Professor I.J. Good, OH, worked as a code breaker at Bletchley Park.

The war also caused financial problems. Fewer boys meant reduced fee and grant income. The cost of the damage caused by the October 1940 bomb was estimated at just over £18,000. By March 1941 the Blitz had partly destroyed the Hoxton estate and the tenants had fled from many of the remaining houses, so between 1940 and 1942 the Charity's income fell from £13,000 to £6,000 a year. During 1942 Barclays Bank asked the Governors to provide security for their overdraft, and Barclays' Metropolitan Manager insisted that the Master of the Company, Sir Maurice Jenks, engage accountants to produce a report on the Charity's finances. Faced with a joint deficit of some £13,000 for the Acton and Hampstead schools, the Governors almost closed both, but after the Board of Education allowed them to concentrate further the Charity's income on them rather than the two Hatcham schools, the Master and four Wardens persuaded Barclays to grant a £15,000 overdraft.

The 1944 Education Act saved the situation. Schools with an adequate endowment could opt for Direct Grant status. This was a continuation of the 1907 system as modified in 1926. If a fee-paying school allocated 25% of its annual entry to freeplace pupils paid for by LEAs, the Ministry of Education would give it an annual direct grant for every pupil aged over 11. The Governors reluctantly accepted voluntary controlled status for the two Hatcham schools. Faced with a choice of complete independence or Direct Grant status for Acton and Hampstead, they preferred independence, but they knew it would lead to an increase in fees, and the Ministry advised that it would be irrevocable, whereas if they choose Direct Grant status they could opt for independence at some time in the future. They thus opted for the Direct Grant, and on 16 August 1946 the two schools received another Scheme.

The change gave the Governors an opportunity to rationalise their own organisation. Since 1873 the same board had been responsible for four schools, two in Hatcham and, after 1898, one in Acton and one in Hampstead. From 1946 the two voluntary controlled schools at Hatcham remained attached to the Haberdashers' Company but were governed separately from the Direct Grant schools at Acton and Hampstead. The new arrangement recognised that the two pairs of schools differed markedly in situation and character, but not for some years was it argued that similar differences implied a common board but separate local committees for each Direct Grant school.

8

Dr Taylor and Hampstead

1946–1961

During December 1945 and January 1946 the Governors reduced a 'long list' of 28 applicants for the post of Headmaster to a 'final list' of four, who were assessed for qualifications and performance when re-interviewed on 15 January. After careful and lengthy consideration of two closely matched candidates, the Governors appointed Dr Thomas Whiting Taylor.

Born in 1907 and educated at the Merchant Taylors' School in Crosby he had gone up to Christ's College, Cambridge, on an open scholarship in classics, graduated with a first class degree, won the Burney Prize for Philosophy, and been awarded a PhD. He had spent 1931/32 at Frankfurt University and also taken a Bachelor of Divinity degree from London University. He was widely experienced. He had taught classics to the sixth form at Bradford Grammar School, Handsworth College and Worksop College, and spent six years as Headmaster of the City of Bath School.

He took over at Hampstead on 1 May 1946 and attended his first Governors' meeting on 10 May. He faced daunting challenges. Damage at Hampstead led to a claim of £17,550 to the War Damage Commission but repairs, and some modest changes and improvements, were not completed until 1948. As late as October 1948 building operations led to morning assembly being held in the playground during fine weather. The year 1947/48 resulted in a current account deficit of £1,103 and by March 1949 it had grown to £7,988. When in January 1950 a staff deputation asked for an all-round salary increase of £100 to meet the high post-war cost of living, there was still a deficit of £5,000 left from 1949 so the Governors were obliged to refuse, whatever their personal feelings.

Hampstead, 1950s.

Sixth form dance, 1946.

BELOW LEFT: Lower School boys at Hampstead, 1950s.

RIGHT: Prep boys at work.

Aged only 38, Dr Taylor was younger than most of the staff, and although a fluent German speaker he had done no war work, and had not shared the perils of the Blitz. The old guard were therefore wary of him, but he avoided conflict and worked subtly to gain control. He found the school was bomb-damaged and pervaded by 'a smell of concrete stairs and cabbage', as his wife Margaret still recalls. John Lear, one of his former pupils at Bath, whom he invited to teach at Hampstead, remembers that the smoke wreathed Masters' Common Room had a 'distinctly Dickensian feel, an open coal fire, with oars crossed on the walls', and that the Manual Training Room, which had been closed during the war, and which John Lear was to turn into an innovative Craft Centre, was used to store the fuselage and wings of a Gypsy Moth aeroplane, until the RAF mercifully removed it.

However, Dr Taylor was energetic, enthusiastic and forward-looking. He organised a sixth form dance and made himself available to all pupils and teachers alike. He aimed to diversify and widen the curriculum, to raise further the school's academic and cultural standing, and to use its metropolitan base to establish a national reputation. In September 1946 he began subsidiary and general studies courses and appointed a Director of Music, Dr McLellan, who travelled up each day from Hove. At the end of the autumn term he challenged post-war austerity and raised staff morale with a lavish Christmas Lunch, still remembered by John Lear. During 1947 he took on a full-time Chaplain and moved the carol service to St Martin-in-the-Fields on Trafalgar Square, after which he invited the

ABOVE LEFT: Post war ski trip. RIGHT: The Corps. Dick Hewson and Wilf Hewitt, 1950s.

staff and their families to a sumptuous tea. He thus overcame the suspicion of long serving teachers and attracted the goodwill of younger ones, and as professional relations became less formal he was eventually known by his first name, as were his successors.

School activities multiplied. In 1946 John Dudderidge resumed his canoe trips to the Norfolk Broads. At Easter 1947 'Uncle Jeff' Cooper ('Josh' Blunt's successor as head of the Lower School) took 14 boys on a holiday to the south of France, and in August five boys spent a fortnight studying at the City University in Paris. In 1948 Dick Hewson took a group on a ski trip to Switzerland, and M.J. Grabow, a sixth former, spent August 1949 staying with a German family in Hamburg. At the start of April 1948 the War Office amalgamated the Junior Training Corps (army) with the Air Training Corps (air force), forming the Combined Cadet Force (to which a navy section was added in 1950). Dr Taylor responded by establishing the Special Service Unit (now School and Community Service) and made the Corps voluntary, although the enthusiasm of Dick Hewson and Wilf Hewitt ensured it survived.

Some of the Governors felt that Dr Taylor's proposals to send teachers on refresher courses, and on foreign exchanges, to employ ever more of them, and to introduce new subjects, were too expensive. In July 1947 W.R. Clemens (an old boy of the Hoxton school, later commemorated with the Clemens Memorial Prize) suggested reducing the number of teachers. In December W.C. Brett (another Hoxtonian governor, who gave his name to the Brett Study Hall) was shocked to find sixth formers having dancing lessons in the Hall, so in February 1948 he persuaded the Governors to immediately and unanimously ask Dr Taylor why he had allowed such a thing without their permission, and to request that it be stopped. Matters came to a crisis as the record deficit emerged early in 1949.

Meeting on 15 March the Finance Committee decided that Dr Taylor must not spend more than £10 without the permission of the Company's Clerk, must keep stricter control of the petty cash book, and must state the cost of special subjects 'not strictly within the

Dr Taylor, Headmaster, 1946–73.

Canoe club at Monmouth, 1953.

curriculum of a grammar school'. At a meeting held on 25 May the Governors held 'A general discussion ... upon the condition of the school, both as regards general organisation and the discipline of the boys and upon the matters raised at the Finance Committee ... and it was unanimously resolved to ask the Headmaster to tender his resignation and failing his resignation being received to give notice to him to relinquish his office.' However, the minutes record that on 9 June 'After a full discussion the explanation given by the Headmaster was accepted and the matter of his resignation be not pursued.'

After this crisis, the Governors and Headmaster had a better relationship, helped by the fact that Colonel P.C. Bull took over as Chairman of the Governors in March 1950 and Commander H. Prevett as Clerk to the Company and Governors in May. Colonel Bull, a veteran of the First and Second Wars, an academic chemist who lectured at Imperial College, a devout Christian and loyal Freemason, an ebullient and extrovert man, was in many ways the exact opposite of Dr Taylor, but they made a strong team. Colonel Bull saw that the short-term way out of the financial crisis was through Direct Grant and fee increases, the former almost a third of the school's income. Fortunately, in September 1948 the Ministry increased the Direct Grant capitation award from £16 to £20 per eligible pupil, and in February 1950 allowed the school to raise the fees from £39 to £60 a year. Thus the Governors were able to consider longer-term policies, and during 1950/51 sold the Kent estate and re-invested the capital to generate a higher and more stable rate of return.

Colonel P.C. Bull on the 50th anniversary of the School's move to Hampstead.

Margaret Taylor recalls that when Tom returned home to Bath after being interviewed, he said 'If I get the job, I'm going to move the school', but at that time circumstances were against a move. He found that it had been the Governors' policy to consider a move since before the war. In June 1946 they asked him to move the re-established Preparatory Department to Chase Lodge, and in May 1947 he did so, freeing space at Hampstead for older grant-attracting boys, as had been done in 1921. In February 1949 the Governors considered moving the whole school to Chase Lodge, in May the Ministry of Education's inspection report stated that Chase Lodge was 'a more suitable site', and during Speech Day in July Dr Taylor said that he hoped to move the school there. However, the Governors concluded that the site was too small, so declined to draw up detailed plans. Instead, in 1951 they bought St Michael's School in Flower Lane, Mill Hill, and in May 1952 established a fully fledged Preparatory School there, calculating that it would pay its way with 150 pupils. In fact, at the end of the financial year 1952/53 both the Hampstead School and the Preparatory School were in surplus, allowing modest expansion and refurbishment at Hampstead.

The inspection held in October 1948 was a personal and professional triumph for Dr Taylor, if less so for the school at large. The report's verdict on his role as Headmaster was: 'He brings to this task high academic qualifications, and considerable teaching experience … The Inspectors were all very favourably impressed, not only with his quick grasp of the school's problems, but also with his tact and firmness in dealing with them.' He assisted in teaching German and Greek, but specialised in religious instruction in the VI and V Forms, on which the report judged: 'It is a privilege for the senior boys to receive this instruction … at the hands of a fine scholar and a skilled teacher who has the gift of adapting his wide learning to the needs and understanding of his pupils.' Issued by the Ministry of Education on 27 May 1949, two days after the Governors had resolved that he would resign or be dismissed, the report doubtless influenced them when they reversed their decision on 9 June.

The statistics published in the report showed how the school had changed since 1932. It now had 735 boys and 39 teachers. The proportion of boys from Middlesex had increased to 82%. The proportion of 11+ entrants receiving free places was 22%. The report does not provide figures on social background, but it is possible that the fact that 51% of the 11+ entrants were from public elementary schools (increasingly called primary schools) indicates some dilution of the school's middle class clientele. Thirty- three boys who left the school in the three years before 1932 had gone to university, and 30 did from 1946 to 1948 (although the post-war figures were untypical and incomplete because of the effect of the war itself and of National Service).

Preparatory School at Flower Lane, 1953.

Gymnasium and assembly hall at Hampstead.

Chemistry laboratory, 1950s.

Open Day, Art Room, 1959.

The inspectors considered the assembly hall, gym, art room and library much too small, as were the cloakrooms and kitchens. They considered that the Headmaster's plan to introduce a five-year course for the School Certificate Examination would help to raise standards, if combined with more innovative teaching and thorough marking. They felt that 39 full-time masters was too few, but came close to damning them with faint praise:

> The academic qualifications of the staff are adequate if undistinguished; it is surprising in a school of this size and standing to find only one Master with a First Class Honours degree. Only three of the staff showed outstanding ability as teachers in their own line; most of the others, however, are thorough and efficient in the work, though there is room for a good deal more enterprise.

They recommended raising the school's 'special responsibility' allowances 'to attract good and highly qualified teachers'. The report concluded:

> The keen competition for admission and consequent high standard of ability amongst younger pupils suggest possibilities of a high and, indeed, distinguished standard of achievement. The encouragement of such a standard by enterprising and enlightened teaching is, therefore, the most important task which now confronts the school.

That advice coincided with Dr Taylor's ambitions for Haberdashers'. The main school at Hampstead was soon buoyant. In 1952 there were 700 candidates for 140 places and a total of 840 boys, so the number sitting the new Ordinary Level GCE and entering the sixth form was higher than ever before. Extra-curricular activities continued to flourish. The Sociological Society and Railway Society took pupils on visits throughout England.

In 1954 Dr Taylor arranged an exchange with Emden High School, and four German boys broadcast their impressions of England on BBC radio's Children's Hour. In 1955 the Rowing 1st VIII represented London in a regatta held for youth teams in Heidelberg, where they found the people 'surprisingly amiable and helpful'. In 1956 John Lear built a set of moveable scenery and he and Dr Taylor took *Julius Caesar* on tour to West Germany, where it was performed to packed houses. Margaret Taylor recalls that several tours between then and 1972 were equally successful. During Commendation Day in 1958 Sir Edward Boyle, Parliamentary Secretary to the Ministry of Education, rightly called Haberdashers' 'one of the first flight of Direct Grant schools'.

Sport was exceptionally strong in the 1950s, benefiting from coaching by first class sportsmen amongst the teachers. John Dudderidge, who introduced generations of boys to canoeing, not only represented Great Britain in canoeing at the 1936 Olympics in Berlin, but attended every Olympics between then and 1996, either as competitor or official. Dick Hewson, who joined the school in 1938, was a Cambridge Boxing Blue. David Thomas, Director of PE 1948–68, played hockey for Great Britain at the Melbourne Olympics in 1956, where A.E. Robinson OH was a member of the British water polo team. In 1960 Michael Palmer (the only man ever to win three successive Varsity cross-country championships) who taught English was a member of the 3000 metres steeplechase squad at the Olympics in Rome, where Victor Matthews OH competed in the hurdles.

Influenced by celebrations held to mark the fiftieth anniversary of opening the new school in Hampstead, in December 1953 the Governors had set up a Site Sub-Committee, in February 1954 it concluded that it was 'desirable to find a new site' and by the end of March had persuaded the Company, which 'agreed to it in principle'. In 1955 Dr Taylor reminded the Governors exactly which parts of the Hampstead premises the inspectors had believed to be inadequate, and stressed that 'The chief need is to find a new site in the country.' As in the 1890s, it was not easy to find a suitable one. During April 1956 the Site Sub-Committee negotiated with Lord Aldenham to take a 12-months option on a ten-acre

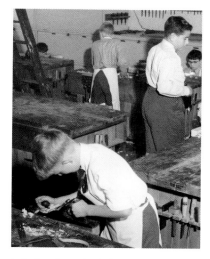

Junior boys in woodwork class.

BOTTOM LEFT: Railway Society trip to Derby, 1950s.

RIGHT: Sociological Society visit to colliery in Kent, 1951.

Rugby at Chase Lodge.

Cricket: going into bat at Chase Lodge.

site adjoining Stanmore Station. In May W.R. Clemens heard rumours that in two years' time the BBC was likely to put Aldenham House, near Elstree, and its surrounding estate of about 100 acres up for sale. His information was correct. In May 1958 the Governors learned that the BBC had decided to sell, so informed the Company, which approved their intention to buy 'with enthusiasm', and so moved quickly, negotiated over the £37,500 asking price, and on 9 February 1959 bought Aldenham House and 61 acres of land for £31,000. (They rejected Lord Aldenham's offer to sell them an adjoining 150 acres because they thought his price of £50,000 'exorbitant'.)

Financial and other planning had begun in 1956, complicated by the fact that new building was still going on at Hampstead, in 1957 costing £12,350. The Company's architect, James Caldwell, calculated that the cheapest possible new school (including a hall with two sides entirely of glass, and without a dining room) would cost £350,000 and estimated the total cost of the project at about £480,000. The Governors hoped to provide £245,000 from selling the existing buildings and land, to borrow £130,000 and to raise over £100,000 from a public appeal. Colonel Bull, still Chairman of the Governors, and now also Master of the Company, laid the foundation stone at Elstree at 3.00 p.m. on 29 October 1959. The Charity Commissioners then issued yet another Scheme, which on 27 November 1961 changed the school's name to 'The Haberdashers' Aske's School', thus recognising that it had left Hampstead and implying that it was the pre-eminent Haberdashers' Aske's school, superior to those at Hatcham and Acton. Colonel Bull died early in 1960, but is commemorated by the P.C. Bull Memorial Prize, awarded to each year's School Captain.

OH reminiscences of the school in the 1940s and 1950s are as prolific as those of the inter-war years. Brian Sewell, the art critic, a pupil during the Second War, recalls that there 'were aspects of school life for which I remain deeply grateful, rugger and cross-country running high among them, both of which served me well in the army' but confesses that he still struggles 'to cast aside all bitterness and perhaps discover an episode that did not involve spiteful and repressive masters or sexual adventures with my peers'. However, he does admit that Locke, a History master 'grave and dry', he 'enthusiastically respected', and Lewin, a 'sympathetic English master', he 'almost loved'. (Dr Taylor also had a high opinion of Roy Lewin and in 1947 made him Head of the Preparatory School.)

Opinion about masters varies. Professor Andrew Booth (1931–37) recalls 'Harry' Payne in the 1930s as:

An absolutely splendid teacher and the kindest of men. I remember the only time I saw him chastise a boy. The boy, W—n, was a well-known lout and a bully. He was very large and heavy whilst Payne, though burly, was quite short. W—n was insolent to the extent of rudeness on one occasion and virtually threatened Payne if retribution was exacted. We were all petrified as to the outcome but Payne calmly went over to W—n's stool, picked him up by his collar and threw him into the corridor, telling him never to come to the class again!

Emeritus Professor John Holmes recalls Payne in the 1940s 'rather fondly as another hazard to be negotiated in the process of growing up' but remembers his faults too; such

Painting of Aldenham House, early 1880s.

CLOCKWISE FROM TOP: Entrance hall 2007; Peter Hamilton, Headmaster, chairs Prefects' Meeting; memorial window to Roy Lewin in Preparatory School Library.

Music. CLOCKWISE FROM TOP LEFT: Junior recorders; jazz band; orchestra recital.

FACING PAGE: Boys on Ski Trip, 2006.

THIS PAGE: Annual Art Trip to the Henry Moore Foundation. INSET: Art Visit to Paris, boys in front of the Eiffel Tower.

ABOVE: Break time — Middle School boys and girls from the neighbouring Haberdashers' Aske's School for Girls.

RIGHT: Junior boys at break time.

ABOVE: Boy sketching in Picasso Museum, Paris 2001. ABOVE RIGHT, FROM TOP: Boys in Monet's garden, 2000; A-Level art.

The Preparatory School. CLOCKWISE FROM TOP LEFT: Playground cricket; clay modelling; Library; pre-Prep class.

as creating an air of tension by springing surprise tests, prodding boys with 'his dreaded metre stick', giving them apt but unkind nicknames, and occasionally using his 'very sharp and ready wit' in a way that showed he 'enjoyed humiliating the unfortunate boy who had stepped out of line, and the latter's fear and discomfort transmitted itself to the whole form'.

Lord Brittan, the former Conservative MP, Chief Secretary to the Treasury, Home Secretary and Vice-President of the European Commission, a scion of Haberdashers' in the 1950s, is more measured in his memories. He recalls being an ambitious boy who valued the school because it gave a recognisably good education without dominating his life. It had a distinct character and a certain formality, so the masters wore gowns, and the boys were forbidden to eat in the street, but it was not noted for particularly harsh discipline. Locke and Moody were impressive History masters, but the teacher who most impressed him, and influenced him to read English at Cambridge, was Nicholas, who affected a slightly unconventional air and non-establishment ethos by wearing a corduroy jacket. Lord Brittan enjoyed his time at the school, particularly as a member of the Debating Society, and took part in the Dramatic Society's 1954 production of Ibsen's *An Enemy of the People*,

Staff inspect a model of the Elstree School. Left to right: Dudderidge, Oliver, Knight, Dr Taylor, Pook, Barling and Crossman.

Scenes from the ceremony to lay the foundation stone at Elstree, 1959.

1690   1959

HABERDASHERS' ASKE'S SCHOOL
THIS STONE WAS LAID ON 29TH OCTOBER 1959 BY
LIEUT-COLONEL PHILIP CECIL BULL. D.S.O. T.D.
MASTER OF THE
WORSHIPFUL COMPANY OF HABERDASHERS
AND CHAIRMAN OF THE SCHOOL GOVERNORS.

COMMANDER H PREVETT. O.B.E. R.N.   T W. TAYLOR. M.A. PH.D. B.D.
CLERK TO THE HABERDASHERS COMPANY.   HEADMASTER.

CAPTAIN C.S.B HICKMAN. O.B.E. R.N.   J E L CALDWELL. F.R.I.B.A. A.M.T.P.I.
CLERK TO THE SCHOOL GOVERNORS.   ARCHITECT.

Ibsen's *An Enemy of the People*, 1954. Phillip Oppenheimer on the right.

playing Aslaksen, the Chairman of the Ratepayers' Association, opposite Phillip Oppenheimer's Stockman. *Skylark*'s critic noted: 'L. Brittan also produced some bold effective acting. He made very good use of his voice, never wasting a word.'

Simon Schama, Professor at Columbia University, New York, the well-known author, broadcaster and historian, a pupil at Hampstead and Elstree, was awarded a starred First in History at Cambridge and immediately elected to a Fellowship at Christ's College. He remembers only three bad teachers: 'One was a monster. I actually hated another two who took pleasure in humiliating kids.' However, he also had fine History teachers: Bob Baynes, a 'really great teacher, he was really wonderful' with the gift of infusing a dingy classroom at Hampstead with the atmosphere of Victorian political debate; Robert Irvine Smith's classes on the Enlightenment 'were fantastic, he looked like Voltaire, sounded like Voltaire'; Ian Lister 'treated us like grown ups'; and Roy Avery was 'incredibly warm hearted and exuberant'.

Alan Bennett's stage play *The History Boys*, for which Schama has written a preface, catches something of Haberdashers' atmosphere and mentions the school by name. Bennett's fictional Headmaster reflects on his own school's status: 'We are low in the league. I want us up there with Manchester Grammar School, Haberdashers' Aske's. Leighton Park. Or is that an open prison?'

Schama's own post-war generation at Haberdashers' included some very able men, besides Lord Brittan. Sir Martin Sorrell, founder and chief executive of WPP, the world's second largest advertising group, was Schama's contemporary at school (Captain of cricket in 1963) and at Christ's College, as was Sir Nicholas Serota (Captain of the 1st XV and School Captain in 1964), Director of the Tate Gallery. Michael Green knew them at school, but left at 17, founded his own business and eventually became chairman of Carlton Communications and ITN.

Peter Oppenheimer achieved distinction as an economist at Christ Church, Oxford, and in the early 1980s was one of the leaders of the movement to ensure that Mrs Thatcher, a fellow Oxonian, was not given an honorary degree. Peter Collins became Fellow and Tutor in mathematics at St Edmund Hall, besides being the college's Cellarer and an expert on Alsace and its wines. Michael Lipton took his degree in PPE at Balliol College, but did not stay in Oxford, in 1994 becoming Professor in the Poverty Research Unit at Sussex University. On the other hand, in 1993 John Skinner moved to Oxford, as Consultant at the Radcliffe Hospital and Dean of the Faculty of Accident and Emergency Medicine.

Keith Edelman had a varied and successful career in business, in 2000 became managing director of Arsenal FC, and for some years was a school Governor. Miles Templeman is now (2007) Director General of the Institute of Directors. Another contemporary, Thomas Harris,

Some OHs, left to right: Sir Nicholas Serota, Simon Schama, Michael Green.

was knighted for his public-spirited and untiring work as Consul General in New York in the aftermath of the 11 September 2001 attack on the World Trade Center. David Pearce, the best-selling architectural author and historian, who died in 2001, bequeathed funds for a scholarship at Haberdashers'. Philip Ward, a prolific travel writer, turned his talents to fiction and in 2003 published his first novel, *The Comfort of Women*. He has recently been joined by Doug Watkinson, a scriptwriter for TV detective series including *Lovejoy*, *Z Cars*, *Poirot* and *Midsomer Murders*, who has adopted the pen-name Marcus Barr for the publication of his own first novel *Haggard Hawk*. He testifies that 'Haberdashers' was a lovely school, liberal yet disciplined, free thinking – but they inspired you'.

They joined the pre-war generation of prominent OHs who made their names in the 1950s and 1960s. John Bambrough had already made his mark at Oxford. Lionel Kochan was on his way to being what his obituary in *The Independent* (27 October 2005) called 'one of the most significant Jewish historians since the Second World War'. A.E. Green, the first of 'Pop' Oliver's pupils to win a scholarship at Jesus College, Cambridge, became Professor of Applied Mathematics at Durham University, from where he was elected a Fellow of the Royal Society. Alan Charig was not only Russian Interpreter with the Control Commission in Germany (1946–48), but as Curator at the Natural History Museum became an internationally respected expert on dinosaurs, and wrote and presented the ten-part BBC TV series *Before the Ark*, screened during 1974.

Professor Paul Freeling, OH.

After taking a brilliant degree in mechanical sciences at Queens' College, Cambridge, in 1943, Paul Wolff played an important part in developing jet engines and gas turbines, and was a key figure in the UK's atomic energy programme, although he received more publicity by rescuing Harold Wilson from drowning in 1973, thus changing the course of British political history. Haberdashers' also educated a clutch of academic medics. Professor Paul Freeling was one of a handful of doctors who revolutionised general practice in this country in the second half of the twentieth century. Professor John Scales was largely responsible for the creation of biomechanical engineering, which allowed the developments of artificial joints. Professor Robert Horton was a pioneer in the field of vascular surgery, using grafts to save legs from amputation.

Paul Daneman, OH.

In contrast, Air Chief Marshal Sir Theodore McEvoy received the Sword of Honour at Cranwell and won promotion in the Royal Air Force but had not attended university. Nor had the most commercially successful OH of the pre-war generation, who wisely kept his name and business interests out of the limelight, and after generous anonymous donations to the school died still worth £78,000,000. Paul Daneman's degree in Fine Art from Reading was less important to his 40-year career on the stage and in films than the fact that in 1955 he appeared in the English premiere of Samuel Beckett's *Waiting for Godot*.

Two members of the generation educated in the 1930s seemed to have a foot in almost every camp. After a triple starred First at Cambridge, the Indian Civil Service, Lever Brothers, Unilever and the Confederation of British Industry, from 1969 to 1972 Maurice Zinkin worked as unpaid Professor of Management Studies at Bradford University. Sir Henry Phillips distinguished himself at London University, survived the fall of Singapore, the Thailand–Burma Railway and a Japanese prison, joined the Colonial Service and was appointed to the first Cabinet of newly independent Malawi, before returning to Britain in the 1960s and making a new and highly successful career in business and commerce.

9

Transformation at Elstree
1961–1973

The real work of moving the school from Hampstead to Elstree took place only after the foundation stone had been laid. Tom, as Dr Taylor was now usually known, planned well. During 1959 he bought a famous Willis organ from Hove town council, to enliven morning assembly. In 1960 he announced that in future all boys would receive an even sounder education by taking most of their O Levels after five years not four. Early in 1961 he appointed Keith Cheney the school's first full-time librarian, with the task of moving the library from its new but relative small accommodation at Hampstead to more spacious quarters at Elstree, where he ran three successive libraries, the latest of which, the Bourne Library, contains not only specialist study, careers and ICT rooms, but the sturdy handmade library tables which were brought from Hampstead.

When 'Pop' Oliver retired in 1960 Tom divided the Second Master's duties between a Second and a Senior Master, appointing respectively 'Bill' Crossman and Otto Pask, and giving the former the job of planning and supervising the move. How do you move a school? John Carleton, who was appointed to teach chemistry in 1960 and retired as Second Master in 1998, recalls:

In our case we did much of it ourselves. In the Summer Term of 1961, after the exams were over, senior boys and members of staff packed books, paper, art and craft materials, even chemicals and apparatus, and dismantled benches and plumbing from the physics laboratories, on to the back of an open 3-ton lorry, sat themselves on top of the boxes and were driven out to Elstree. When the lorry had been emptied, we went back for the next

Building works at Elstree, 1959-61.

load – this took many days, even with final help from a fleet of removal vans for the really heavy items. Not only did these activities save money, but the pupils and staff working together in this joint venture derived pleasure and a real sense of satisfaction that their efforts were helping to create their new home.

On 11 October 1961 the Lord Mayor of London opened the new school. His visit was marked by another foundation stone, and closed-circuit television was used to transmit the ceremony from the hall to a marquee in the grounds. (The 1959 foundation stone and the 1961 stone are now side by side in the porch leading to the Bourne Hall Foyer.) In fact, the school's accommodation seemed likely to be barely adequate, since it had become clear that although Aldenham House could contain a Boarding House, it was too small and too unsuitable for the many other facilities which had been proposed for it, including an arts and crafts room, six other full sized classrooms and the Headmaster's living quarters. Fortunately for Tom and his family, the Governors agreed to provide a house in the grounds, and it was built according to designs prepared by his wife Margaret.

Although the term began a fortnight late, the assembly hall was not ready so, weather permitting, assemblies were held in the playground, with Tom speaking through a loud hailer. The Preparatory School (7 to 11 year olds) had rejoined the main school, but it shared accommodation with the Junior School (11 to 13 year olds) in what was sometimes called the BBC Block, since it had been built and used by the BBC during the Second World War. Music was housed in two classrooms and a small office over the assembly hall foyer, quarters so cramped that the musicians rapidly if not enthusiastically colonised window-less stores under the hall balcony. In 1959 the Governors had decided: 'The Sixth Form Block should be the central feature of the new buildings and should include

Organ in situ at Hove.

Leaving Hampstead, summer term 1961.

The official opening of the new School at Elstree, October 1961.

adequate Sixth Form rooms grouped round the Library.' Yet there never seemed to be enough rooms, and lessons were taught in the wings of the hall stage and in the Boarders' Reading Room in Aldenham House.

John Carleton remembers that

> Science and practical subjects (art and pottery, metalwork and woodwork) had their own dedicated classrooms, but most other subjects were taught to Middle School boys (14 to 16 year olds) in 12 general-purpose classrooms situated around the cloakrooms and kitchen. They were designed in six pairs, with large sliding doors to enable each pair to be opened up to form a large area for House assemblies. However, the doors were not very soundproof, so boys sitting at the back of one room could listen to their own lesson and the one in the next room. At lunchtime the sliding doors were opened and the rooms were used as House dining rooms, one for each of the six Houses. The catering staff wheeled in heated trolleys from which they served the meals. House prefects cleaned up and rearranged the rooms for afternoon lessons, but teaching usually took place with the aroma of cooking lingering in the air and pieces of squashed vegetable on the floor.

The Lord Mayor unveils foundation stone at Elstree, October 1961.

Many members of staff found that teaching there in the first period in the afternoon was a hazardous and sticky experience, making frequent trips to the dry-cleaners an occupational necessity. Nor was the situation entirely satisfactory for the boys, since the food seemed not to travel well between kitchen and classrooms. Peter Barry, who arrived in England with his younger brother John in the summer of 1972 to begin a two year stay while their father served in the Canadian High Commission, has vivid memories of the new diet:

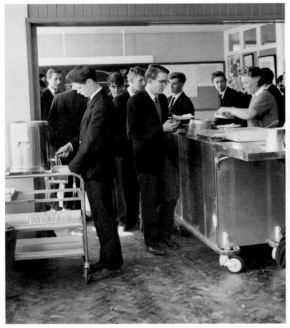

ABOVE LEFT: Serving lunch from heated trolleys in a House dining room.

RIGHT: Dr Taylor taking assembly in the playground at Elstree, 1961.

Cast of *Twelfth Night* on West German tour, 1969.

Our first week at Habs. was a blur, but we do have fond memories of gracious masters and welcoming new school chums. Our first lunch, however, was an experience we remember with less enthusiasm for this is when we met new friends named 'Spotted Dick', 'Yellow Peril' and 'What the — is that?' To this day we are not sure how it happened but we soon became used to the local cuisine and we dedicated ourselves to the great fun that was Habs.

Without John Rolfe's work as Transport Officer many boys would not have reached Elstree at all. In 1961 a small number of coaches served only four pick-up points and stopped outside the main gates both before and after school, for the present extensive coach park had not been built. Indeed, the roads and lanes around the school were so quiet and peaceful that about 100 boys and staff cycled to school, leaving their machines in the extensive bike sheds. So remote did the school seem to some of the bus drivers that Richard Ambor, who had sat the entrance exam at Hampstead, and so was one of the original intake in Hertfordshire, recalls 'school buses full of pupils shooting round the countryside looking for Elstree'.

The school was organised on a House basis, each House being a forum for activities and a haven for pastoral care. Each had not only its own double room, but an adjacent cloakroom and office, although the latter were also departmental offices, causing some overcrowding, and persuading many teachers to gravitate to the Staff Common Room. Tom equipped it with a billiard table, rightly thinking that it would make the SCR a focus for social life, especially so since light refreshments and newspapers were available there. Changes were legion. Rowing, fostered by Tom in 1946, was ultimately a casualty of the move. The annual Gilbert and Sullivan opera soon withered in the rural air, but music and drama luxuriated in the assembly hall, which had a fly-tower and stage fit to rival many theatres, and grew ever more polished and successful. Most sports, freed from the tiresome journey between Westbere Road and Chase Lodge, benefited enormously. Not all the initiatives endured. Archaeological excavations led by Professor Swinnerton (Tom's father-in-law) were eventually abandoned, bee keeping was deemed too dangerous to continue, and the School Press did not long survive the departure of its mentor, Lawrence Broderick, now a highly successful sculptor.

Tom did, however, make lasting changes to the sixth form curriculum by introducing General Studies, and in 1962 hosted the National Conference that founded the General Studies Association, which almost inevitably elected him its first chairman and Irvine Smith its first secretary. Aware of the changing temper of the times, he also made crucial changes amongst the teachers. J.G. Knight, who had taught science with great distinction since 1925, retired in 1964; Peter Keevil, an inspirational art teacher since 1928, in 1965; and John Dudderidge in 1966. When 'Bill' Crossman and Otto Pask retired in July 1964 Tom appointed Roy Lewin and Dai Barling Second and Senior Master. When Roy Lewin died suddenly in 1968 Dai Barling ('Taffy' to the boys) became Second Master and Leo Guidon Senior Master, the former to discipline the boys, the latter to manage the staff, which he did with consummate diplomacy and tact. A memorial window to Roy Lewin is in the Preparatory School Library.

Encouraged by the 1963 Robbins Report, which recommended the expansion of higher education, Tom recruited teachers to specialise in sixth form work and coach the growing number of Oxbridge candidates. His vision for the school, and his gift of choosing the best teachers, included the confidence to give them freedom to teach in ways that were appropriate to them and to their pupils. He retained them by salaries, fair treatment and generous conditions of service. The Staff Dining Room, in which each teacher had a personal linen napkin, retained waitress service and each table had a menu card, frequently offering a difficult choice, on Fridays often between Dover and lemon sole. The teachers developed a fine sense of esprit de corps, not always easy for new-comers to appreciate, but seen at its best in a willingness to go the extra mile, and at its most vociferous at the Christmas Lunches, high-spirited feasts during which the lucky ones found the traditional silver 3d. bits concealed in their pudding.

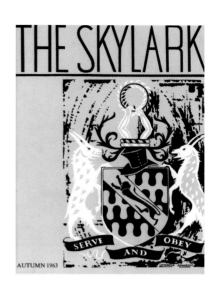

Cover of *Skylark* designed by Lawrence Broderick.

BELOW FROM LEFT: Peter Keevil, art teacher, Leo Guidon, Broderick in the art room.

Tuck shop, 1961.

Basil Flashman teaching Prep boys.

Things were different behind the scenes. In the first months at Elstree spending was high and in March 1962 the School Governors proposed an 'expenditure freeze'. They wanted the Company's new Clerk, Commander Prevett, on the spot at Elstree to control expenditure. He complained of lack of liaison between the Company (as Foundation Governors) and the School Governors and suspected that financial control was inadequate. Assisted originally only by 'Pop' Oliver and by Miss Pridmore (the redoubtable school secretary, 1928-1969) Tom handled all accounts. In January 1963 the Governors decided that 'Dr Taylor's authority for payment is limited. He has no authority to overdraw', and attempted to cap expenditure by resolving 'The Clerk is authorized to remit, monthly, to the Headmaster, the sum of £3,300.'

In June the Clerk presented a report to the Governors' Financial Sub-Committee. The school had borrowed £27,500 from Barclays to pay for unanticipated capital expenditure, current expenditure was £12,000 above the agreed figures, and there was a deficit of £7,858. The school had begun the financial year short of 44 day boys, eight boarders and one preparatory boy, so its revenue was inadequate. He concluded 'Elstree now faces a financial crisis of the first magnitude, and unless immediate and drastic action is taken, there is a possibility that it will have to close before the end of the year, through the impossibility of finding money to pay salaries and wages.' Tom 'agreed that the financial situation was extremely serious'. He could not agree to reduce expenditure by accepting the Clerk's suggestion of forgoing three masters, but would limit spending on books and equipment, and in September would increase entry by 60 boys (in the event, by 50).

In July the Governors agreed to the Clerk and Headmaster's joint proposal that as a temporary measure the Clerk should work as a Bursar at Elstree, and that a full time Bursar would be found as soon as possible. In November they agreed to the Clerk's own suggestion that instead of the existing single governing body for the Boys' School at Elstree and for the Girls' School at Acton, there should be one central body to coordinate two local committees, one for Elstree and one for Acton. At the end of May 1964 the Elstree Governors investigated the school's 'whole administrative set- up' and drafted a

Financial Directive on the exact duties of Governors, Headmaster, Clerk and Bursar, J.E. Burrough, who had taken up his appointment at the beginning of the month. In September he presented the Governors with proposals for improved accounting procedures, and little by little rationalised spending.

The Governors had been made all the more apprehensive by the knowledge that from 10 to 18 October 1963 the school was to be inspected by the Ministry of Education. This time the inspection report praised not just Tom but the whole staff. The Headmaster 'has done excellent work, and shown devotion to every aspect of school life and willingness to experiment.' The 65 full-time masters included 12 with first-class degrees: 'A school like this needs men of high quality and it seems to have them. The staff is of high calibre.' There were 'very good relationships between Masters and boys', the 'House system works excellently', the 'boys are lively minded, vigorous and full of enterprise', and 'Music and Drama are outstanding'.

The report praised the 'wisdom and courage of the move' from Hampstead to Elstree, noted that total numbers had risen from 735 to 1071 (and in the sixth form from 111 to 290), that at 11+ there were five or six applicants for each place, and that the 'system of selection is good', so that 90% of the boys entered the sixth form and 60% of them left with two or more A Levels. In contrast to the findings of the 1948 inspection, 43% went to university. However, the report suggested that the O Level results could be improved and brought up to the standard of the 'very good' A Level and Oxbridge results. Compared with four open awards at Oxford and Cambridge from 1946 to 1948, the school had won 29 between 1961 and 1963.

Nor was the report uncritical of the accommodation, almost brand new though it was. The assembly hall, PE, art and practical design facilities were believed to be excellent, as were the kitchen and staff common room. However, it considered the 11 laboratories too few and too small, the library and sixth form rooms too small, deemed that English, geography, history, maths and modern languages needed subject bases, and felt that the

John Lear teaching metalwork, 1961.

The swimming pool and gymnasium at Elstree.

Opening the cricket pavilion, Colonel Fraser Bird on left, 1965.

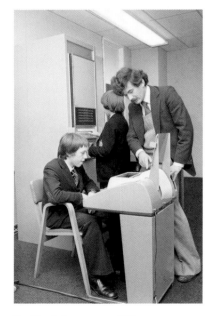

The School's first computer, 1972.

Plaque in the music school.

Preparatory School merited 'separate provision'. These recommendations influenced the school's development for the next 40 years.

Despite the Clerk's disturbing report, in June 1963 the Governors had agreed to estimates for the academic year 1963/64 which predicted expenditure of £175,000 and income of £185,000 yielding a £10,000 surplus, and in December 1964 bought 40 acres of land from Lord Aldenham, significantly extending the school's site. Buoyed up by the inspection report, and aware that the school was £13,148 in credit, in January 1965 the Governors decided to build a new library, to construct specialist rooms for arts subjects and to provide a second science block. As always, the problem was how to raise the money, estimated at £150,000. The Clerk suggested closing the Boarding House, which was making a loss, and using Aldenham House as a Sixth Form Centre, thus releasing space in the main school, but Tom persuaded the Governors to reject the idea.

Confidence was raised during 1965 when Colonel Fraser Bird met the entire cost of a cricket pavilion, an act of generosity commemorated by the annual Fraser Bird Match. Fund raising plans were drawn up during 1966, and in July 1967 a mammoth fete opened a building appeal so successful that the foundation stone of a new library was laid in September 1968. During May 1969 Princess Margaret (an Honorary Freeman of the Haberdashers' Company) toured the school, and Sir John Wolfenden (who had been taught by Spilsbury at Wakefield) opened the new Library in September. The original Library became the Sixth Form Common Room, which it remains today, although the new Library later became the Modern Languages Centre, and was replaced by the present Bourne Library.

Inflation accelerated in the middle 1960s so the building fund lagged behind rising costs until December 1969 when an anonymous donor (soon to be referred to in gratitude as the Anonymous Donor) offered £35,000 towards the library and £25,000 towards a Science block, and in January 1970 offered £150,000 towards an Arts block, dwarfing the £70,000 accumulated by the Governors, and putting the £323,000 post-inflation total cost of the whole project within reach. Building continued and in September 1971 Mrs Thatcher (the Secretary of State for Education) opened what were prosaically called Phase II and Phase III, the former containing specialist classrooms for geography, physics and technology, the latter for English (including a Drama Room), history, modern languages and maths. Early in 1972 a member of the Company gave £6,200 for a Hewlett Packard Mini-Computer, one of the first in a British school, enthusiastically used by Douglas Whittaker, Head of Maths. (Curiously, Phase II and Phase III were the only buildings whose opening was not marked by a foundation stone or plaque.)

With characteristic drive and foresight, in February 1972 Tom told the Governors that the new buildings had so much 'improved the teaching facilities' that the school should immediately plan for new preparatory and music blocks. Barely a year later the Anonymous Donor promised £400,000 towards them, suggested calling the latter the 'T.W. Taylor Music School', and determined that it should have priority. No one from the Company or the school met the Anonymous Donor until 1974, and he guarded his privacy with some success, so although the Music School's Seldon Hall was named after his solicitor, the story behind the name remained a secret.

ABOVE LEFT: Princess Margaret's visit, 1969.

RIGHT: Mrs Thatcher being interviewed by pupil in Headmaster's study, 1971.

However, by the time the Music School was built Tom had retired. Just before the Governors' meeting on 29 November 1971 he had had a private conversation with Colonel Fraser Bird and Major General Sir John Bates (the Foundation Governors), and by the next meeting on 12 December had submitted a letter announcing his retirement as of 31 August 1973. He attended his last Governors meeting on 13 July 1973: 'Dr Taylor thanked the Chairman and Governors for their help and encouragement throughout the last 27 years' and 'The Chairman and Board expressed their sincere and personal thanks'.

A series of tributes and presentations to Tom and Margaret Taylor had begun in March 1973 with a gala concert at the Royal Festival Hall, and marked the atmosphere of mutual goodwill and respect in which he completed his years as Headmaster. It was a fitting tribute to his concern for academic excellence that in November the school gained its best Oxbridge results to that time, 22 scholarships and exhibitions compared with the ten of 1960. Bruce McGowan, who had taken over as Headmaster in September, told the boys that Dr Taylor might properly be regarded as the school's second founder, and announced that he would be commemorated by the T. W. Taylor Music School whose construction was to begin in 1974. A plaque and a bronze bust of Tom by Lawrence Broderick are set within a rail to the left of its foyer.

Inevitably, Tom was not free from some possibly carping criticism about his attitude to discipline and the time that he gave to his many out-of-school commitments. However, the majority of teachers, especially the younger ones whom he had appointed and often inspired, appreciated his individuality and verve. Now retired themselves, they look back to a more relaxed time when Tom seemed capable of bearing any burden and solving any problem, when a quick and rhetorical 'All well?' from him might be followed by a welcome promotion or salary increase.

The boys could find him a little pre-occupied and withdrawn, but he had an almost mythical status with them, renowned not only for many individual acts of kindness and understanding, but for granting a half holiday when his son was born, buying an early colour TV to watch the moon landings, and dutifully saying 'Goodbye' to each leaver in his study. Perhaps OHs remember him best casually opening his letters on the stage before morning assembly began, giving a pious talk including one of his favourite aphorisms,

Plaque and a bronze bust of Dr TW Taylor by Lawrence Broderick.

THOMAS TAYLOR
HEADMASTER 1946 – 1973
THIS BUST WAS CREATED BY
LAURENCE BRODERICK
HEAD OF ART AND DESIGN
1961-1981

Boys on the Quad around St George, a sculpture by Lawrence Broderick.

Skylark editors on front cover, left to right: Simon Alterman, Paul Infield, Felix Mara, Mike Fischer, Chris Auty, Mark Rawlinson and Andrew Machallam (holding gun).

'Moderation in all things' and 'To thine own self be true', or smiling alertly and enigmatically as the school sang Jerusalem and To be a Pilgrim in excited and often stifling end-of-term assemblies as sunlight streamed in through the then glass-sided walls of the hall at Elstree.

In retrospect, it is clear that he was a shy but gregarious man with a quicksilver mind, detached but humane, fully known only to a few intimates, but with a wide circle of admirers and friends who gave him their confidence and to whom he gave wise counsel. He was an educational administrator and pioneer of the greatest distinction. He believed that the pursuit of academic and cultural excellence produced civilised behaviour, and deprecated the need for formal and traditional punishments, although he was prepared to use them when necessary. The move to Elstree was not only the turning point of his life's work, but so accelerated Haberdashers' development that it enabled the school to challenge and overtake long established and nationally known public schools. Despite all the changes that have taken place since 1973, Haberdashers' remains recognisably Tom's creation.

The 1960s were notable for radical changes in social aspirations and behaviour, and in political ideas and principles. The impact affected schools as much as any other sector of British life. The Campaign for Nuclear Disarmament attracted many boys, and at Commendation Day in 1962 a group heckled Sir Theodore McEvoy, who claimed that CND was run by Communist agents and traitors who should be put up against a wall and shot. In March 1968 sixth formers wrote to the Minister of Education objecting to the school's new rules on long hair, an episode reported in the *Evening Standard*. After a noisy demonstration in the Quad Tom, who kept resolutely to the 'short back and sides' of his youth (and so was nicknamed 'Spud'), met the protestors and adroitly explained that the new rules were in fact more liberal than the old. He then set up three Advisory Councils. On 2 December 1970 the Sixth Form Council voted to ask him to relax the dress regulations for a trial period, and during the second half of the Spring Term of 1971 Sixth Formers were allowed to relinquish school uniform, provided its substitute included a jacket, neck-wear and sensible trousers. Dai Barling, a pacifist by conviction but a disciplinarian in practice, discreetly relaxed the school rules, and corporal punishment, already rare, became very rare indeed, as he based discipline as far as possible on common sense, cooperation and self-control.

Yet an atmosphere of rebellion persisted. In September 1971 a letter in *Skylark* claimed: 'School uniform is part of a process designed to destroy the individuality of the student, which is itself incompatible with the demands of an authoritarian system requiring unquestioning obedience.' Andy Goff, an American pupil at Haberdashers' during the late 1960s and early 1970s, has the fondest memories of his 'British education', but at the time his brother Rory wrote: 'There is often a feeling of oppression. Though this is a mistaken feeling, it does point to a situation in which the teachers are thought to be estranged from the students.' In the early 1970s it was correctly rumoured that an OH was a member of the Angry Brigade which bombed the homes of two Conservative cabinet ministers: John Davies, Trade and Industry Secretary, and Robert Carr, Home Secretary, who lived in nearby Hadley Wood.

School election, 1970.

Some sixth formers regarded Che Guevara (the Cuban revolutionary) and Mao Tse-tung (the once-revered Communist Chinese leader) as freedom fighters to be emulated by anarchic subversion. Richard Berman, then so hirsute that he deflected criticism by wearing a short-haired wig, but now a Cambridge graduate and hedge-fund manager, believed that 'we were questioning the establishment consensus, trying to secure various freedoms; political, social and educational'. He and his friend Mark Klimt issued a fortnightly magazine, named after a Rolling Stones song, *Street Fighting Man*, objecting to corporal punishment and parodying the attitudes and methods of unpopular teachers. Other sixth formers tried to provoke and unsettle the teachers by spiriting garden gnomes on and off prominent parts of the school buildings and grounds. One group used weedkiller to incise the message 'Spud Taylor FO' in the grass on the Quad, where its traces lingered for many years.

David Griffiths, who was appointed to teach history in 1968 and retired as Head of Sixth Form in 1996, recalls that in the 1970s in particular

> Haberdashers' was often a place of laughter. The essence of Haberdashers' wit was the ability to think laterally, to relate a comment or action to something other than what was originally intended. For instance, at Commendation Day in 1971, Mrs Thatcher, then Minister of Education, described the age, size and venerability of the Haberdashers' Company, and then turned to its Master, of whom her phrases were a perfect description, at which point the sixth form, ensconced in the balcony of the assembly hall, exploded with laughter, much to her obvious surprise.

However, perhaps the most notorious example of Haberdashers' humour occurred in December 1972 when a group of sixth formers concocted a letter, purportedly from Tom's newly announced successor introducing himself to the parents. Amongst other things, Bruce McGowan's supposed letter told them that he was 'a firm believer in Keynes', of plans for 'a close relationship' with a German school named after the Nazi hero Horst Wessel and situated in Berchtesgaden, the site of Hitler's Bavarian hideaway, and asked them to pay in advance if they wanted their boys to have 'French lessons' at a riding school near Elstree. The spoof was discovered only when some naïve but dutiful parents sent the school cheques for the stipulated £69.

10

Consolidation

1973–1987

Born in 1924, Bruce McGowan was a pupil at King Edward's School, Birmingham, where his zeal as school captain earned him the nickname 'Nimrod' (the mighty hunter). Between 1943 and 1946 he was with the Royal Artillery in India and Burma, and in 1947 took his BA in history at Jesus College, Cambridge. From 1949 he taught history and Latin at King's School, Rochester, and in 1953 became Head of History at Wallasey Grammar School. In 1957 he was appointed Headmaster of De Aston School, Market Rasen, and in 1964 moved on to be head of Solihull School. From 1968 to 1970 he was also a member of the Public Schools Commission.

Thus when Bruce, as he liked to be known, arrived at Haberdashers' in September 1973 he had a wealth of experience at his disposal. He believed in putting the right person in the right job. Only two heads of department left the school in his time, but resignations and retirements allowed him to appoint younger House Masters. When Dai Barling retired in 1982 some of the Second Master's disciplinary and pastoral duties were given to the new post of Head of Middle School, intended to coordinate and support the form tutors. Bruce enjoyed exercising patronage: Solihull old boys were appointed to teach English, history and religious studies; members of Jesus College were promoted to be Head of Careers, and of Lower and Middle School.

He knew that Haberdashers' local and national reputation was based on its academic excellence. He also knew that one of the foundations of a successful school was good organisation. He issued a new prospectus, cultivated links with local preparatory and primary schools, had reports printed on both sides of the sheet (to allow teachers to give fuller

Inter-House Sports Day at Elstree.

B.H. McGowan, Headmaster, 1973–87.

advice), separated Upper Sixth from Lower Sixth Parents' Evenings (to the same end), and put the master-in-charge of general studies in charge of subsidiary subjects as well (to improve attendance). After John Carleton succeeded Dai Barling as Second Master in 1982, Bruce appreciated his administrative and organisational skills and supported his policy of producing a termly Fixture Card, which contained a calendar of events (to minimise clashes and excuses) and a clear table of assemblies (to lessen early morning confusion), and of introducing a staff handbook (to establish clear professional standards).

The first major problem Bruce faced was to recruit new teachers. During the late 1960s and early 1970s teachers' salaries lagged behind the cost of renting and buying property within travelling distance of Elstree. The Governors could not agree on a solution, for example declining to buy nearby property or to build in the school grounds. Matters came to a head in 1973, for 17 teachers left with Tom, proving very hard to replace. When a number of posts became vacant for January 1974 Bruce advertised three times to find anyone to interview, let alone appoint. He therefore persuaded the Governors to introduce removal allowances, which met estate agents' and solicitors' fees, so made it easier for existing property owners to move into the area. For a time the school leased a house that it sublet to newly arrived teachers, so they could save before buying locally. (Bruce's successor, Keith Dawson, persuaded the Governors to provide bed-sits and flats in Aldenham House.)

The school lost a fund of experience as veterans of the Second World War retired – 'TEC' Carrington (in the 1950s apt to use a pillory and a truncheon to overawe his classes), Nick Clarke-Lowes (an artillery officer with the Eighth Army in North Africa), Tommy Sanderson (a veteran of the Italian campaign), Frank Smith (captured by the Japanese in Burma), and 'Auntie' Willatt (who had served in India, and whose special quality was recognised by his colleagues and friends who later funded two memorial prizes). Fortunately, members of a younger generation took the lead and school drama, music and sport flourished as never before. Under Stephen Wilkins' expert direction school plays continued to rival West End productions in innovation, quality and verve. As

BELOW, LEFT TO RIGHT: Hockey team, 1987; Cross Country running and high jump.

a very diplomatic and well-organised Director of physical education, David Davies coached the 1st XV to 65 unbeaten matches from October 1973 to December 1977, a record that will surely never be equalled, let alone overtaken.

Conducted by Alan Taylor, who had succeeded Dr McLellan as Director of Music in 1962, school choirs, concerts and orchestras reached ever-higher standards, and helped to confirm Haberdashers' national reputation for all-round excellence. Haberdashers' choir made its debut at The Royal Opera House, Covent Garden, in 1972 and sang in every production of *Carmen* from 1973 to 1996. In fact, in the 1975/76 season the choir recorded *Carmen* with Sir Georg Solti and the London Philharmonic Orchestra for Decca. For some 20 years Alan Taylor conducted the choir at the Royal Albert Hall Carol Concerts, and the Good Friday performances of Bach's *St Matthew Passion* at the Royal Festival and Barbican Halls. Leon Lovett, conductor of the London Oriana Choir and English Baroque Choir, commented 'What makes Haberdashers' Boys' Choir so outstanding is that Alan Taylor is able to harness their energy and let it explode in their singing with a subtle purity of tone and disciplined brio of one of the finest vocal ensembles imaginable.' In 1982 Alan Taylor's achievement was recognised when he was rightly awarded an MBE.

Bruce gave his full support. Shortly after joining Haberdashers', he instituted a weekly seminar for new teachers, and visited a lesson given by every teacher, not to inspect, but to learn and to empathise. He attended almost every play and concert, and afterwards entertained convivially and generously, enthusiastically assisted by his wife Pat, well remembered as a brilliant cook and fine hostess, in the seemingly ever-open Headmaster's house. In every Monday assembly he paid close attention to the games announcements and copied the results into his Fixture Card. An ex-rugby referee, he and Pat accompanied two of the school's sports tours to the Far East and mixed confidently and easily with players and guests alike, using their authority and tact to smooth over any problems. Whenever he could he looked in on school trips, and took some himself, particularly on the cruise ship SS Uganda, which became a hospital ship in the Falklands campaign. (A memorial plaque to Lt. Nicholas Taylor OH, a Royal Navy Sea Harrier pilot, who was sadly killed on active service in the Falklands on 4 May 1982, is in the School Chapel.)

In September 1974 the Haberdashers' Aske's Girls' School moved from Acton to a site next to the Boys' School at Elstree. Sheila Wiltshire, the Headmistress, considered that the Girls' School was a rather an 'old-fashioned family school' in comparison. She felt that some of the boys initially adopted a 'patronising' attitude, shown when they coined the pejorative acronym 'HAGS', which led her school to adopt a new name, The Haberdashers' Aske's School for Girls. However, she had excellent professional relations with Bruce. They decided that the two schools would share coaches, foreign exchanges and visits, concerts, orchestras and plays, and sets in sixth form general studies, but keep almost all other things separate. This allowed the schools to engage in mutually beneficial cooperation and rivalry, whilst retaining their distinct character and ethos. In Sheila Wiltshire's view it achieved 'the best of all worlds for both of the schools' and stimulated the Girls' School to emulate the Boys' School's quality and success. When she retired in 1991 and was awarded an OBE she regarded the honour as a compliment to and recognition of what the Girls' School had achieved. Indeed, it was shortly to overtake the Boys'

David Davies with pupils.

BELOW: John Carleton and Alan Taylor, both long-serving members of staff on their retirement.

Junior boys at break.

School in the GCSE and Advanced Level league tables. Her successor persuaded the Governors to recognise the equal status of the two schools by changing the Boys' School's name from The Haberdashers' Aske's School to The Haberdashers' Aske's Boys' School.

Bruce and Sheila faced the challenge of independence together. Between 1965 and 1970 both schools were confronted by a higher Burnham Scale and London Allowance for teachers' salaries, increased pension payments, the Selective Employment Tax, and accelerating inflation. The Ministry of Education refused to raise capitation grants, or to let the schools raise fees enough to break even. It was also reluctant to change the Direct Grant rules: the grant depended on the number of pupils in a school on 31 March each year, but by then sixth formers studying for the Oxbridge exams in the previous term had left. Despite the Bursar's best efforts the Boys' School made a current account loss in the financial years 1968/69 and 1969/70, and had a large overdraft.

The Governors' minutes record that on 18 July 1969 'The [Elstree] Committee therefore recommends that a detailed examination should be made of the financial possibilities of abandoning Direct Grant status and becoming independent.' On 2 December 1969 the Governors decided that if the Public Schools Commission, set up by the Labour government in 1968 and chaired by Lord Donnison, recommended that Direct Grant schools cease to charge fees, then Haberdashers' would choose independence. Early in 1970 the Donnison Report actually recommended abolishing the entire Direct Grant system, but the Labour government narrowly lost the June general election, allowing the Governors to breathe again.

Local politics were also finely balanced. The London Government Act of 1963 abolished the LCC and Middlesex County Council, so LCC and Middlesex Governors were replaced by one representative each from the Inner London Education Authority (ILEA) and the LEAs of Barnet, Brent and Harrow, whose party political balance was volatile. In 1970 the ILEA told the school that it would refuse free places after September

BELOW LEFT: Sculpting with clay; RIGHT: Model Railway Society.

Preparing for Open Day on the Quad.

1971. Other LEAs accepted 50 places for September 1973 and 57 acceptances were expected for September 1974, but because the Direct Grant regulations still stated that to receive the capitation grant a school must admit at least 25% free place holders, with an intake of about 150 boys at 11+ each year, Haberdashers' was quite near the borderline.

However, applications from fee-payers were strong (in 1973 some 300 for 54 places at 7+ in the Preparatory School, and 500 for 150 places at 11+ in the main School). Moreover, after lobbying by one of the Governors, Anthony Sheridan, early in 1971 Mrs Thatcher had raised the Direct Grant capitation from £32 to £62 a year, and amended the scales for fee remission, so the school was within the reach of many more parents. Thus at that point the school's continued Direct Grant status seemed assured and its financial problems less pressing.

Circumstances then changed. After the Conservatives lost the general elections in February and October 1974, the Labour government abolished the Direct Grant system in 1976, and the Governors chose independence for both the Elstree schools. As a member of the Public Schools Commission Bruce was in an ideal position to advise them. A joint appeal raised £420,000 to fund Haberdashers' Bursaries. In 1981 Bruce and the Governors welcomed Mrs Thatcher's Conservative government's Assisted Places scheme, and in the same year Haberdashers' topped the only schools' league table existing at that time, the one for open exhibitions and scholarships at Oxford and Cambridge, with 26 awards, beating Eton College into second place.

The transition to independence was eased when the government reduced the top rate of income tax, by the Governors' new Property Committee (which sold most of the Charity's remaining Hoxton estate, further diversified its investments, and steadily increased its income) and by further improvements to the school's facilities. Aided by the Anonymous Donor, in 1977 two squash courts were opened, and in 1978 the then little-used fives courts were replaced by a climbing wall, partly financed by a generous parent. During 1979 the Sixth Form Common Room was equipped with a cafeteria. In 1980 Princess Margaret opened the Bates Dining Hall (named in honour of Major General Sir John Bates, Chairman of the Governors), ending the practice of serving the boys' lunch in the House Rooms and marking the demise of waitress service for the teachers, although their separate dining room remained inviolate. (A plaque commemorating Princess Margaret's visit is just inside the main entrance to the Bates, as the Dining Hall is usually known.)

The school had a lasting cultural and intellectual influence on its pupils. David Lidington, now MP for Aylesbury recalls Sixth Form English lessons:

Breakfast in Bates dining room, 1980s.

Michael Fitch was a strict and demanding teacher but in his Sixth Form class you quickly realised that behind the formidable outward manner there lay a deep love of English literature and a passionate commitment to share those riches with his pupils. Looking back, my English lessons in the Lower Sixth were one of the most important cultural influences on my life. We read the set books, and of course returned to them in detail in the Upper Sixth, but we also tasted poetry, drama and novels which otherwise I might never have encountered and to which I have returned again and again. In many ways Michael's lessons were the most intellectually challenging that I have ever experienced.

David Lidington well remembers school music:

As a treble, you were given no choice. If you had a reasonable voice, you had to attend choir practice on Tuesday and Thursday lunchtimes. Yet when our voices broke, there was never a shortage of volunteers to sing tenor and bass. It was partly the opportunity to sing great music in exciting venues: Antony Hopkins' *A Time for Growing* at the Royal Albert Hall, the *B Minor Mass* in Berlin, Mozart's *Requiem* in the concert at the Royal Festival Hall to mark Dr Taylor's retirement. Partly, it was the fact that the tenors and basses were treated by the staff in the choir as semi-adults, though I recall one concert in which three basses who had earlier been lubricating their vocal cords in the 'Waggon and Horses', falling backwards off the tiered seats during a particularly exciting bit of Handel. Above all, the willingness of older boys to sing was down to the inspirational leadership of Alan Taylor as Director of Music.

David Lidington was aware of a generational shift occurring in the school, as more old-fashioned, authoritarian teachers, who had taught his father at Hampstead, retired and were replaced by a younger generation, including David Griffiths, Dick Norton, John Wigley and Stephen Wilkins, each of whom fostered debate and discussion in class. 'Haberdashers' was very much a school that encouraged you to ask questions, and challenge received wisdom, particularly in the Sixth Form. I think that's what made the school so special.'

Creative tension between the old and new generations gave boys access to many different personalities and traditions, but occasionally the tension was a little too palpable for comfort. David Lidington recounts that:

Sixth Form Physics lesson, 1970s.

Bruce brought with him a new chaplain, David Scott. David was young, charismatic, won the Sunday Times national poetry competition, and tried to demonstrate theatrically what Christianity meant to him and ought to mean to his cynical congregation in the assembly hall. For one assembly, we all filed in to be greeted by a pile of very large cardboard cartons piled up in front of the stage. A few minutes later, we were treated to the school chaplain bursting out of a carton to the strains of Roger Daltrey singing 'I'm Free'. David Scott's approach to religion was very different from that of the Second Master, 'Taffy' Barling, a Christadelphian from South Wales. The tension showed. A dramatic (and mildly outrageous) Scott assembly one day would be followed the next by a Barling assembly featuring a long didactic passage from one of the more obscure crannies of the Old Testament.

Dai 'Taffy' Barling.

Eventually, David Scott pushed things a little too far. He opened his 'sermon' by saying that the essence of Christianity could be found in Mike Batt's 'Wombling Song': that to 'pick up the pieces and make them into something new' was what we were called upon to do. That would have been OK, but David, in an early experiment with karaoke, put a record on the player and led the school in a mass chorus of the Wombling Song. 'Taffy' Barling did not join in. Halfway through the chorus, the needle got stuck. Most of the school collapsed with laughter. Bruce, his face royal purple, left the stage with as much dignity as he could muster, with the chant 'underground, overground' still being repeated over the loudspeakers. David Scott fled after him. Thereafter, Leviticus ruled.

David Scott, a man of deep compassion and humanity, is now Director of Spirituality in the Diocese of Winchester.

The school's eclectic style did not suit everyone. Rodney Gascoyne felt that average and less able boys could be neglected in the classroom and be given inadequate career advice. Many sixth formers appreciated the erudition of some members of the older

BELOW: Dave Wrench (left) and Douglas Yeabsley (right) at Sports Day. BOTTOM, LEFT TO RIGHT: Barry Goater, Alan Wood, Tommy Sanderson (left) and Keith Dawson (right), 'Yogi' Stewart.

generation of teachers, such as 'Auntie' Willatt, 'a great man and a great teacher', whilst others warmed to the younger men. Some able boys were impressed by 'Yogi' Stewart's background and personality, by his wide literary culture, and by his memorable classroom technique, but others found him just a little too exotic. Hamish Adam preferred being taught English by 'get you through Hanbidge', who acquired his early nickname because he taught lower sets so thoroughly and so well. Douglas Yeabsley was a hero to many sportsmen because 'he never talked down to anyone and had a rare gift for leadership'. Dave Wrench (in 1964 selected for the England XV to play against France and Scotland) and Alan Wood were 'good eggs' – they understood and sympathised with boys of all ages.

Once the cultural upheavals of the 1960s had been assimilated into suburban life some boys were unsure where the behavioural boundaries lay in school itself and could over-react to reproof and punishment. In the mid-1970s the *Skylark*

Hurdling at Inter-House Sports Day.

editorial team so resented Dai Barling's ever-milder disciplinary regime that they included prose and poetry that covertly spelled out the message 'FO Taffy'. After a post-play party had gone a little too far, at least one angry sixth former suspended by Bruce contacted the popular press, which ran an alarmist story. In the early 1990s sixth formers who wanted a separate sixth form car park complained to The Times that the school threatened their human right to freedom of movement.

A feature of pupil–teacher relations was many teachers' ability to deal with high spirits both effectively and tactfully. Jonny Bucknell recalls his surprise when his efforts to suspend a large soft-toy spider over the stage during an end-of-term assembly elicited Taffy Barling's amused cynicism rather than instant punishment. Lance Anisfeld still smiles when he remembers how his economics set collapsed into hysterical laughter because they couldn't understand their teacher's rich Irish accent, but that he joined in and won their respect. Robert Silverman relishes the memory of a teacher reacting to an inebriated sixth former not with disciplinary outrage but by taking the precaution of fetching a waste bin and then letting him sleep it off during the lesson: 'It was one of those moments that all who were present will never forget. A definitive "Haberdashers' Moment".' Sobriety certainly improved after 1983 when the Carol Service moved from St Martin's to St Albans, putting sixth formers out of range of Leicester Square and Soho.

11

Old Boys, Boarding House, Preparatory School

1960s–1980s

The acres of grassland and woods on the Elstree estate gave Haberdashers' a new and more spacious existence. Aldenham House, approached through ornate gates and up sweeping tree-lined drives, impressed all who saw its mellow brickwork and stately interiors. The Boarding House attracted the social cachet of more traditional public schools. Estate, Aldenham House and Boarding, the new teaching accommodation, and shortly the new Preparatory School, influenced Haberdashers' atmosphere and character. They provided an exceptional environment for teaching and learning, stimulated the curricular and extra-curricular work of pupils and teachers, and produced a new image of the school, moulding parental and public perceptions so that its name bore all the connotations of excellence and success. The move from Hoxton to Hampstead was completed by the move from Hampstead to Elstree.

The ablest boys flourished, so the school produced many academics. Simon Baron Cohen is now Director of the Autism Research Centre at Cambridge University. Jeremy Black is Professor of History at Exeter University. Robin Franklin is Fellow and Tutor in Veterinary Medicine at Pembroke College, Cambridge. George Garnett is Fellow and Tutor in History at St Hugh's College, Oxford. Lawrence Goldman is Fellow and Tutor in History at St Peter's in Oxford and editor of the Oxford Dictionary of National Biography. Neil Greenham is Fellow and Tutor in Natural Science at Clare College, Cambridge. After reading English at Pembroke, Malcolm Guite is now Chaplain of Newnham College, Cambridge. Tim Huxley is Senior Fellow at the International Centre for Strategic Studies. After Trinity College, Cambridge, and a lecture-

Aldenham House and grounds being used as a film set
for the nearby Elstree studios, 1960s.

TOP: Simon Baron Cohen.

ABOVE: Raj Persaud.

BELOW RIGHT: Cover of *Warfare in the Western World 1882–1975*, by Jeremy Black.

ship at Durham, Arnold Hunt is Curator of Historical Manuscripts at the British Library. Andrew Scott was a Fellow of All Souls College, Oxford, before becoming Professor at the London Business School.

In 1979 the team from Sidney Sussex College, Cambridge, which won the BBC's University Challenge, contained two OHs, David Lidington MP and John Gilmore, who now specialises in translation studies and Caribbean studies at Warwick University. In 2007 Raj Persaud and his brother Avinash are both Professors at Goldsmith's College, Raj of Psychiatry and Avinash of Finance, almost certainly a unique distinction for one family and one school.

Nor was achievement limited to academia. In 1996 Damon Hill was ambitious and determined enough to follow in his late father's footsteps as Formula One World Motor Racing Champion. Alan Bloom did not apply to university but worked his way up to become a partner in Ernst and Young, and is recognised as one of the UK's top experts in corporate restructuring, having rescued Barings, Canary Wharf and Railtrack. Jerome Anderson turned down a university place in law, entered banking and financial services, then switched careers to become the first FIFA licensed soccer players' agent in the UK, and is now chairman and chief executive of the Sport Entertainment and Media Group. Jerome's son is now at Haberdashers': 'He really enjoys it; he's a better sportsman than I was. But he's also very privileged. Kids have got fantastic opportunities to blossom there, to grow and to learn.'

Simon Shaps read English at Cambridge and rose via reporting for the *Cambridge Evening News* to be appointed Chief Executive of Granada in 2003. Kevin Bakhurst studied Modern Languages at Cambridge and in 2005 was made Controller of BBC News 24. Mark Damazer also went from Haberdashers' to Cambridge and in 2006 became Controller of Radio Four, where he caused controversy by proposing to abolish the channel's theme tune, listened to by a small but loyal audience at 6.30 a.m. Lance Anisfield followed Lord Brittan to Trinity College and the Presidency of the Cambridge Union (Lent Term 1985) and although he put his economics degree and business experience to good use as Special Advisor to Peter Lilley at the Department of Trade and Industry (1991–92), he decided not to enter politics.

David Limb read history at Oxford, and enjoyed a meteoric career in the army, in which he reached the rank of Lt Col., but had commanded 3 Para for barely a single week when he died unexpectedly in August

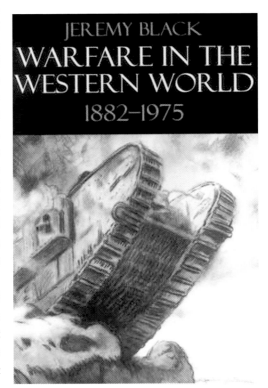

JEREMY BLACK
WARFARE IN THE WESTERN WORLD 1882–1975

Damon Hill at the School, standing second from right.

2000 aged only 39. Teachers and old boys were amongst the many army colleagues who attended his funeral in the chapel at RMC Sandhurst. Unlike David, Richard Harold joined the army straight from school and is now Deputy Governor of the Tower of London.

Jeremy Black remembers most vividly the encouragement given to boys: 'We had so much opportunity to develop, we were given so much freedom.' For Jeremy, the school's greatest legacy to him was its 'intellectual power' – 'twenty-nine boys were sent to Oxbridge from my year. And that was thought of as a weak year – the year before, we had sent 40!' Lawrence Goldman testifies to 'the sheer intellectual stimulation provided by the school' and regards his years there as academically the most exciting time of his life, during which able, competitive and enthusiastic boys with a love of humour were taught in an inspirational, lively and often original way by academic experts such as David Grossel and Stuart Moore.

When George Garnett joined Haberdashers' Fourth Form (now called Year 10) he experienced an 'intellectual awakening' because the academic standard was at least two years ahead of what he had been used to. He enjoyed mixing with clever, interesting and unconventional boys, relished being taught by highly intelligent masters, such as the 'wonderfully entertaining, dry and wry' John Welbourne, all of whom had the highest possible expectations of their pupils. He found the breadth of sixth form work, and the personal freedom as he was tutored for Cambridge, an ideal preparation for university. George believes that 'Haberdashers' was the making of me.' The school gave Raj Persaud his interest in psychiatry, which became his life's work. Raj comments:

Having to deal with the masters as if one were an adult not a boy proved an extremely useful educational experience. I recall that Haberdashers' was a place where high standards were set, but it was also a forgiving place and allowed individuality to develop. I do hope it won't ever change from that.

BELOW: John Gilmore.

BOTTOM: Richard Harold.

ABOVE: Aldenham House was used by the BBC during the war.

BELOW AND FACING PAGE: Photos of Aldenham House taken in the 1920s.

Eric Carlson, a sixth form boarder who read Classics at Cambridge, wrote:

The school was willing to take on promising recruits from the 'awkward squad' who wouldn't stand a chance at most similar schools. This willingness to coach unconventional and nonconformist boys for Oxbridge was one of the best things about Haberdashers', and one of the major features behind its success.

The boarders certainly included a fair share of the unconventional and nonconformist, as Hamish Adam recounted in his Confessions of a Boarder. They also included highly gifted pupils: George Garnett, John Gilmore, Malcolm Guite and Tim Huxley were boarders. George spent three years living and studying in the Boarding House and regards it as 'the most extraordinary institution of which I have ever been a member'.

When the Governors bought the Elstree estate in 1959, built the new school, and adapted Aldenham House for boarders, they knew little of the property's history. Aldenham House originated in a Tudor house called Wigbournes that in the 1620s was owned by Henry Coghill. The panelling in the entrance hall dates from his time, but has probably been repositioned. The Tudor and Stuart house has been concealed by later additions, the west (entrance) and south facades being largely Georgian, and the other, less symmetrical, sides mainly Victorian.

In the 1730s Sarah Hucks renamed the house and built the room now adorned with a portrait of Robert Aske and used as the Headmaster's study. Her son Robert Hucks built the bay window on the south front (now lighting the school office), and the stable yard (which has a date stone of 1785). After his death the house eventually passed to George Henry Gibbs, senior partner in the firm of Antony Gibbs and Sons, director of the Great Western Railway, and patron of the great engineer Isambard Kingdom Brunel. George's widow moved in during 1846, and in 1848 built a billiard room, but died in 1850 leaving the house to their son Henry Hucks Gibbs.

Born in 1819 and educated at Exeter College, Oxford, Gibbs joined the family

ABOVE LEFT: portraits in the library, now the Headmaster's study.

RIGHT: The main staircase.

Lime Tree Walk, Aldenham House Garden, 1924.

Scenes from *The Trial of Oscar Wilde* shot at Aldenham House.

firm in 1843, the year after it had made a loan to the government of Peru in return for a concession to sell guano, a valuable fertiliser, which by the 1860s raised net profits to an annual average of £137,000. In 1850 he had let Aldenham House, but in 1869, the year the Midland Railway opened a station at Elstree, enabling him to commute to the City of London, he decided to move in and restore the house and estate.

During the 1870s the architect William Butterfield provided a Chapel (now the Waiting Room), dining room (the boarders' reading room, now the Chapel), kitchen quarters, entrance loggia and clock tower, etc. His characteristic style marks the Home Farm and nearby cottages. In the 1880s Sir Arthur Bloomfield extended the billiard room into a library (the boarders' dining room, now the Old Refectory). Gibbs enlarged the garden and park to some 200 acres, laid the tree-lined carriage drive towards Elstree, excavated Tykes Water, moved Aldenham Road and New Grubbs Lane (now usually known as Butterfly Lane) away from the house, demolished an ancient public house called the 'Wrestlers' and replaced it with the 'Battle Axes', named after his coat of arms displaying three battle axes which adorns the facade.

From 1875 Gibbs was the senior partner in Antony Gibbs and Sons, which he made one of London's leading merchant banks. He was director and governor of the Bank of England, Conservative MP for the City of London, High Sheriff of Hertfordshire and a Magistrate, dispensing justice from the Court Room, built in 1876 and now a meeting room. An economist, scholar and a deeply religious man, his collection of over 10,000 books included the largest collection of prayer books then existing. He edited the letters 'C' and 'K' for the first edition of the Oxford English Dictionary, and financed the project during the 1880s and 1890s.

Created first baron Aldenham in 1896, he died in 1907, after which his son Vicary Gibbs, assisted by head gardener Edwin Beckett, devoted himself to perfecting one of the most famous and beautiful English gardens. Its ponds and stream still flow into the moat of a medieval house, Penne's Place, whose site forms part of the Cadet Corps' assault course. It included the largest privately owned arboretum in the world, second only to Kew. When Vicary died in 1932 the family decided to dispose of the collection of plants and shrubs, and in 1935 the sale of over 2,000 lots lasted a week. Many rare trees that were too large to move remain in the school's grounds.

In 1934 the house was let for conversion to a health resort, and then as a country club, which in 1940 sub-let to the Ever-Ready Battery Company. In 1941 it was requisitioned by the BBC and used as the home of its South American and Near Eastern Services. Shortly after the war the BBC bought the house and surrounding 61 acres, but in 1956 emptied the house of equipment. The Ministry of Defence decided that it was of no use as a reserve broadcasting station, since both it and the BBC's headquarters in Langham Place would be destroyed in a nuclear strike on London, so the Treasury authorised its sale. When the Governors bought the property in 1959 the house and grounds had to be adapted and repaired. The principal losses were an avenue of diseased and rotten elms whose site became the 1st XI cricket pitch, and the kitchen garden that became the grassed central Quad.

After the school moved in during 1961, the house and grounds were often used by Elstree Film Studios, notably for episodes of *The Avengers* and an eerie black-and-white

ABOVE LEFT: Middle School boarders, 1970s.

RIGHT: Junior School boarders preparing for bed, 1970s.

production of *Village of the Damned* in which the lord of the manor occupies the Headmaster's study, clearly worried by the strange children who are growing up in the nearby village, easily recognisable as Letchmore Heath.

Tom and Bruce loved that study. As parents approached through the entrance hall, crossed the ante-room, and entered the study itself, they were impressed by the Headmaster's status. In Tom's later years his own life-sized portrait (by Lawrence Broderick) on the wall behind him added to the effect, and his reputation amongst the boys was enhanced by rumours that his desk concealed a colour TV that he watched during interviews and meetings. Bruce relished using the room to entertain. Whenever the sixth form current affairs society 'Forum' attracted a distinguished speaker, he offered generous measures of liquid refreshment, and engaged visitors and sixth formers alike in good-natured and relaxed but shrewd conversation, as is recalled by Raj Persaud, one of the society's chairmen.

Tom and Bruce took a particular interest in the Boarding House, watching over the welfare of boys and masters alike. When considering plans for a new school in 1956 the Governors had envisaged a maximum of 500 boys, of whom 120 would live in three boarding houses. By 1959 they hoped merely to fit 100 boarders into Aldenham House, but in 1961 the Ministry of Education stipulated a maximum of 80. The Clerk estimated that 75 boarders paying a fee of £200 a year would yield an annual profit of £1,000, so parents were told that boarding facilities would be provided at Elstree and David Thomas was appointed Senior Boarding Master.

The Boarding House had a difficult start. The fees were set at £180 a year, but with the take-up lower than expected, £210 was needed to break even. The kitchen proved too small, and it was difficult to obtain suitable domestic staff, so from February to June 1962

Mrs Thomas was temporary housekeeper. It was lucky to survive the appalling winter of 1962/63, which tested its electricity, gas and water supplies to the limit. When in 1964 the Bursar's offices were sited in Aldenham House the number of beds available fell to 65, further threatening the viability of boarding, and the Clerk's bid to bring it to an end in 1966 was only averted by Dr Taylor's eloquence.

The Boarding House was often bleak and cold, the facilities few, the food the object of perpetual complaint, and privacy almost entirely absent. More than one former boarder remembers finding a cigarette end in his meal, almost certainly dropped by one of the chain-smoking couple who cooked, and lived in a flat over the former stables, from where the sound of their domestic quarrels echoed round the courtyard. The boarders themselves were a diverse group, seemingly united only by a sense of separation from the rest of the school, and by their own superficially rule-bound way of life, rules which they often found ingenious ways to circumvent.

Eating breakfast and supper in the dining room, attending evening assemblies in the reading room, travelling to Radlett for Sunday morning church, enduring an evening service in the then chapel, storing their personal belongings on insecure shelves, and sleeping in metal-framed beds in brown-linoleum-floored dormitories, was not a way of life many of them would have chosen. Some boys found it difficult to adapt but others such as George Garnett enjoyed a certain distance from their parents, directed any adolescent rebellion against the House, and acquired a confidence and independence that stood them in good stead at university.

The House contained some sources of comfort. Marie Sproat, the permanent housekeeper, dispensed common sense, tea and sympathy from her capacious linen room, and she and her husband Tommy provided supplementary supper in their quarters, so still evoke grateful memories of their kindness. When they retired in 1976 it proved well nigh impossible to find successors of similar quality. The bachelor flat, shared by two young masters, who had to take good care not to be put down for more than their fair share of duties, or be made scapegoats when things went wrong, was a refuge for many boys, supplying coffee, toast and TV, not least on winter Saturday nights when Match of the Day was a popular fixture.

David Thomas and his wife maintained a family atmosphere in their flat, as did David and Jean Davies and their daughters. From 1977 to 1983 David and Flora Griffiths did so too. Flora recalls their years in the House with nostalgia. On their regular Tuesday evening duty, they created a welcoming 'home from home' for one dormitory at a time, providing 'chocolate cakes which seemingly disappeared in seconds'. The boys joined in card and parlour games with alarming intensity: 'I remember well a now-eminent barrister from a very prestigious chambers stomping off upstairs because he hadn't won.' Occasionally the senior boys would slip over the fields to the 'Wagon and Horses' and they sometimes grew a little too daring: 'Our bedrooms were on the ground floor and one night one of the boys had a terrible fright when he knocked on our window instead of our daughter's.'

Declining demand for boarding persuaded the Governors to close the Boarding House at the end of the Summer Term in 1983, but the Anonymous Donor's generosity continued as he contributed money towards the Sime Preparatory School, which was completed in 1982, and which Princess Margaret opened on 30 June 1983. The Preparatory Block was reconstructed as the Design Centre, opened by Sir Monty Finniston in 1984. (A plaque marks each opening ceremony.) The Anonymous Donor also funded the Sports Hall, which was opened in 1985 and named the McGowan Sports Hall (recorded by yet another plaque). Thus Haberdashers' accommodation had been further improved, to the benefit of future generations of boys and teachers.

Until 1982 the Preparatory School had had a chequered history. After the 1875 reorganisation a preparatory class was provided at the Hoxton School, and in 1900 a Preparatory Department for boys aged 5 to 8 was set up in Hampstead, but was closed shortly after the 1921 inspection. In 1924 two of the former preparatory mistresses (Miss Biggs and Miss Challen) set up Westcroft in Cricklewood Lane, an independent preparatory school that henceforth provided many Haberdashers' pupils. Emeritus Professor John Holmes joined Westcroft in 1938 and recalls Miss Biggs as 'tall, well-spoken, elegant and dignified, with her hair in a bun', Miss Challen as 'short, stout and tweedy, with cropped grey hair, the stern headmistress'.

When the Governors bravely opened the Haberdashers' Preparatory Department in the house at Chase Lodge on 7 May 1947 it was barely ready. Boys were taught in the changing rooms whilst new classrooms were built, and there were no kitchens, so two coaches took boys and teachers to Westbere Road for lunch, and then waited to return them to Chase Lodge. In 1952 the larger premises at the former St Michael's school in Flower Lane 'were not quite complete' when the boys moved in, although there was a

Prep art class at Flower Lane, 1950s.

kitchen which provided excellent hot meals. Numbers rapidly grew from 80 at Chase Lodge, to an initial 100 at Flower Lane, and to 140 when the newly-designated Preparatory School was opened officially by John Bambrough in 1953. The school quickly developed a family atmosphere under the benevolent care of Roy Lewin.

In 1961 the Preparatory School joined the main school at Elstree, when the Prep. boys abandoned their grey jackets for the dark blue blazers long worn by the other pupils. Basil Flashman, who had taught at Flower Lane since 1957, was given responsibility for the Prep. boys, at first under Reginald Manning (for some years remembered with the Manning Memorial Library), who was Head of both the Prep. and the Junior School, but from 1966 Basil was independent Head of the Prep. Its quarters in the utilitarian concrete and steel block put up for the BBC in 1940 were not ideal, but dedicated teaching from Mary Geddie and Jo Snaith amongst others allowed the boys to flourish. Basil designed and planned the 1982 building, and its facilities gave full scope to teachers and pupils alike.

Many OHs recall the Prep. sailing trips (accompanied by Basil's wife Margaret, who taught at the Girls' School, and used her pupils as crew), the ski trips to Switzerland (on one occasion accompanied by Graham Hill), or the barge trip down the Rhine from Cologne to Amsterdam (where quite accidentally Basil took the boys on a tour of the 'red light' district). Basil did not hide in his office but taught for 29 periods a week, getting to know every boy in the Prep., and did not keep the parents at arm's length, but invited

Jo Snaith teaching in the 'BBC Block' at Elstree.

Prep. boys going out to play rugby, early 1970s.

ABOVE LEFT: Pam Bryant teaching art.

RIGHT: Designing a poster.

them to cheese and wine parties, and the mums to morning coffee. When he retired in 1989 the Prep. parents gave him a superb evening reception, to which he and Margaret arrived and from which they departed in a specially provided Rolls-Royce, and during which he did a lap of honour round the inside of the assembly hall on his legendary motorbike!

Bruce himself had retired two years earlier. From 1981 to 1984 Bruce chaired the political and public relations committee of the Headmasters' Conference, and in 1985 was Chairman of the Conference itself, a prestigious position that marked the peak of his career. Perhaps he became just a little too fond of making firm executive decisions, for during 1986, at the very end of the meeting at which he announced that he would retire in 1987, he told the assembled teaching staff that he had nominated a former Haberdashers' teacher to the post of Head of Sixth Form. Until that moment they did not know that the post existed. He had not advertised, so neither any outside teacher, nor any serving Haberdashers' teacher, had been able to apply. The latter were outraged. The incident strained relations between Bruce and the staff, relations that unfortunately had not been fully restored when he retired in July 1987. With grim humour, he presented the Staff Common Room with a new Suggestions Book and a bookmark in the shape of a dagger, as he said 'for stabbing people in the back'. Needless to say, they were never used, but were an unfortunate note on which to end an otherwise successful headship.

12

Challenges and Responses
1987–2001

K eith Dawson succeeded Bruce McGowan. Born in 1937, Keith Dawson was a pupil at Nunthorpe School near York, read history at Queen's College, Oxford, was awarded a Diploma in Education with distinction, and in 1961 began his teaching career at Ilford County High School. He had joined the Haberdashers' history Department in 1963, and impressed Tom, who appointed him Head of history in 1965. In 1971 he left to become Headmaster of John Mason School in Abingdon, by 1979 he was Principal of Scarborough Sixth Form College, and by 1984 Principal of King James College in Henley, from where he returned to Haberdashers' as Headmaster in September 1987.

It was a potentially difficult position. After 16 years significant changes had taken place, but 22 of Keith's former colleagues were still teaching at the school. He would have to establish a new working relationship with them and one with the rest of the staff, if possible without prejudice to either group. His former colleagues recalled him as he had been when teaching history at Haberdashers' in the 1960s. During morning assembly he had read his mail on stage, at lunchtime he had eaten early to ensure a place at the billiard table in the Staff Common Room, and it was rumoured that he had once smoked and still drank. He had been an inspiring history teacher, innovative, yet a stickler for disciplined hard work from pupils and teachers alike. Outside the classroom he had coached cricket and hockey, directed school plays, and starred as Jack Worthing in the long-remembered staff play, Oscar Wilde's *The Importance of Being Earnest*, in which Michael Fitch had played Lady Bracknell and Dai Barling the Revd Chasuble.

Combined Cadet Corps.

Keith Dawson, Headmaster, 1987–96.

All this augured well. Between being appointed in 1986 and taking up his position in 1987 Keith visited Haberdashers' many times, sometimes formally – interviewing Heads of Department and Housemasters, and sometimes informally – meeting teachers, pupils and parents. He asked the teachers to call him by his first name, and indicated that he hoped to create a collegial atmosphere of mutual and shared responsibility. In September 1987 he quickly resumed his former high level of activity and involvement. He spent hours on the touchline and boundary, supporting players and their coaches and talking to parents. He attended almost every performance of every play and concert, and visited rehearsals as well. Nor was his dedicated interest confined to Elstree, for he visited school parties elsewhere in the United Kingdom and on the Continent, often making long and time-consuming detours from his family holidays in order to do so.

In 1990 the school's Tercentenary Year (shared with the Elstree Girls' School and the Boys' and Girls' Schools at Hatcham) encapsulated many of Keith's enthusiasms: a thanksgiving service at St Paul's Cathedral, a concert at the Royal Albert Hall, a Families' Art Exhibition, a lavish Sports Day, a special Charity Appeal; and a veritable feast of school music and drama, including a school play and a staff play, Moliere's *Tartuffe*, in which he took part. *Skylark* rightly praised his 'gem of a performance' as Monsieur Loyal. Only the joint expedition to Newfoundland proved too distant to receive his on-the-spot approbation and support.

Keith strongly supported school music and drama. A cellist, he often invited pupils to repeat part of an evening's 'Music in Miniature' at a morning assembly. He ran a number of very successful 'Young Professional' concerts on Sunday evenings, providing a venue for budding musicians, many of them former pupils, and raising money for charity. In 1996 he joined Stephen Wilkins in producing the school play, *The Marriage of Figaro*: *Skylark* recorded that they directed 'with an exquisite eye for detail'. To encourage pupils to participate in and value cultural events, and School and Community Service occasions such as Mencap Funday and the Senior Citizens' Christmas Party, he instituted Honours

The annual Mencap Fun Day at Elstree.

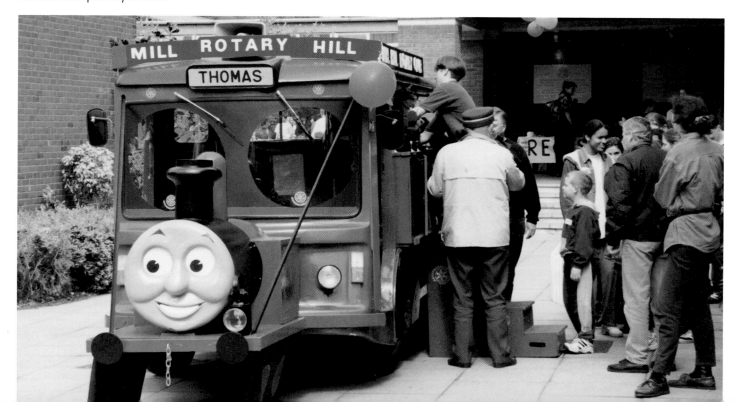

Ties, modelled on games colours, but awarded for exceptional endeavour in non-sporting activities.

He was aware of future challenges about to face Haberdashers' and so strengthened the wider school community, appointing Douglas Yeabsley to support parent social activities and to maintain contact with former pupils. In 1992 he formed a Parents' Social Committee, to promote attendance at extra-curricular activities and to help at school functions. In 1995 he became president of the Old Haberdashers' Association and improved its links with the school, notably by reviving Old Boys' Day (long held in the Summer Term) and instituting an OHA–Staff Dinner (now held annually in the Autumn Term), besides introducing a life membership scheme to improve the OHA's financial position.

He knew that the 1961 buildings had been given an official lifespan of only 25 years, so needed refurbishing or replacing. He believed that the school had to keep abreast of developments in information technology. He considered that each academic department needed its own dedicated and well-equipped teaching rooms. Thus with his vision, and the drive and energy of Mr Gordon Bourne, the Chairman of the Governors, and the generosity of many donors to an appeal, work began on a major new building in July 1991. Many of us remember toasting Mr Bourne in rather good champagne as he coaxed a bulldozer into cutting the first piece of turf.

Work progressed so well that the appropriately named Bourne Building was declared open by HRH Princess Margaret in October 1992. The complex houses a magnificent new School Library, a specialist Careers Library, an information technology department, and (on the ground floor) new accommodation for the classics and history departments, plus a large foyer where pupils' creative work can be displayed. A kitchen and servery facilitate entertainment at concerts and plays held in the upgraded assembly hall.

Other developments followed in the wake of the Bourne. The 1969 Library was reconstructed as the Modern Languages Centre, and was opened by Lord Brittan (under his previous status as Sir Leon, as the foundation stone records) in 1994. English, maths

ABOVE LEFT: Demolition to prepare for the Bourne Building, 1991.

RIGHT: Princess Margaret with Chairman of the Governors opening the Bourne Building, 1992.

Lord Brittan, OH, opening the Modern Languages Centre, 1994.

Staff play, *Forty Years On* by Alan Bennett, 1996.

THIS AND FACING PAGE, FROM LEFT: Sport; rugby, hockey, football, water polo.

and religious studies were provided with self-contained teaching areas, and the rooms occupied by economics and politics were remodelled and extended. Each of the six Housemasters now had an office separate from that of an academic department, and each of the three Section Heads had his own office, making a considerable difference to the level of privacy and quality of discipline and pastoral care. Sport was not neglected. In March 1995 David Thomas returned to open the school's first AstroTurf all-weather playing surface, for hockey and soccer in winter and tennis in summer (as is recorded on a plaque affixed to the gate).

Keith re-established a kitchen in Aldenham House and brought the elegant Old Refectory into use for meetings and receptions. Similarly, he revived the practice of serving cricket teas in the Pavilion, greatly enhancing the social side of matches. Early in 1995 the administration and provision of catering was contracted out, 'smart' cards were introduced for payment in the Bates and at the School Shop, and an even wider choice of food and refreshments was introduced, allowing boys the freedom to 'mix and match' according to their individual tastes and preferences.

Haberdashers' academic quality and standing were Keith's areas of special interest. The school had had virtually the same curriculum since 1961. It now had to cope with the demise of seventh term Oxbridge entrance examinations (1986), the introduction of GCSE (also 1986), and the erosion of the traditional pattern of Advanced Level examinations by course work and modules. To assess these developments he set up his Renaissance Committee, whose name implied that Haberdashers' needed to experience a revival of learning. His approach was to seek consensus and agreement by discussion, diplomacy and goodwill, an approach which brought out the best in people and won their cooperation and consent to policies about which they had initial reservations. When he made it clear that the purpose of staff appraisal was not to judge but to support, even that controversial policy seemed acceptable.

In many respects a school exists independently of its Headmaster. Pupil ability, ambition and energy have obviously long created a common academic experience at Haberdashers'. Much of the school's depth and richness is created by the multitude of extra-curricular activities that Keith did so much to foster, and their true effect is less academic than personal and social. Activities provide enclaves in which are forged bonds of friendship and loyalty hidden from most teachers and many other pupils. Occasionally pupil solidarity can challenge loyalty to the school. Nicholas Levy recalls that at the height of the car park controversy the sixth form enlivened an end-of-summer-term assembly by adapting the words of Jerusalem and singing that their swords would not sleep in their hands 'until we have built a car park in Elstree's green and pleasant land'. No one was surprised when Keith held the sixth formers back and gave them a lesson in good manners.

However, pupils do change. For many years Haberdashers' pupils were a mixture of boys from mainly Anglican and Jewish families. When the school accepted grants from the Board of Education, it informed parents that they could excuse their sons from religious education, and since the lessons were broadly Protestant, Jewish and Roman Catholic boys were withdrawn. In the Autumn Term of 1915 the school arranged for a Rabbi to teach 100 or so Jewish boys on Saturday mornings, but the practice did not survive the First War. Thus Protestants and Catholics were taught separately and Jewish boys not at all, a system that the 1921 inspectors thought anomalous, but during the 1920s and 1930s the school's atmosphere and ethos absorbed differences of background. In the 1940s Brian Sewell, then something of a Catholic apologist, was grateful to Jewish boys 'who had the courage to support my obstinate rebellion against compulsory membership of the Cadet Force'.

During the 1970s non-Jewish and Jewish boys had separate RE lessons, but in Keith's time the school's ethnic and religious composition widened, reflecting the changing composition of its catchment area, boys of Asian origin accounting for up to one third of

Battle of the Bands.

Some long-serving members of staff: Basil Flashman, Mike Anderson and John Rolfe.

Ken Jerred, school porter, 1971–96.

the school. It was clearly inappropriate to teach Buddhists, Hindus, Jains, Muslims and Sikhs a diluted form of Christianity, or to gather them together for an overtly Christian morning assembly, so with the advice and support of the Revd David Lindsay (David Scott's successor as Chaplain) Keith transformed RE into an innovative course in religion and philosophy for all boys, and introduced a voluntary Thursday morning assembly for each faith group, whilst everyone was welcome to attend his own ethically-based assembly in the hall. This arrangement helped to deepen Haberdashers' sense of community, and contribute to the school's tradition of cultural individuality and mutual respect.

Long-serving teachers provide a school with educational and personal continuity, but teachers also change. In the words of Isaac Watts' hymn 'Time, like an ever-rolling stream, bears all its sons away.' In 1988 Leo Guidon and Barry Goater, in 1989 Basil Flashman, in 1994 Keith Cheney, Roger Wakely and Mike Anderson, and in 1995 John Rolfe each retired from full-time duties, in every case after working for over 30 years at Haberdashers'. Inspired by a remark by Dai Barling, who taught at the school for 40 years, Keith Cheney suggested that teachers who had served for at least 100 terms deserved special recognition, and to mark their contribution Keith Dawson established a dining club called 'The Termites'. (The longest-serving member of the school community was almost certainly Bob Packer, a groundsman from 1929 to 1979, as is recorded on a memorial in the Chapel.)

During Keith's final year it was clear that he regarded his two periods at Haberdashers' as the high points of his career. For all the vexation it was capable of causing, he loved the school. He had vastly improved its many facilities. He had proved to be a man of compassion and warmth, always willing to see good in others, and agonised over difficult decisions lest a wrong one be made. He had been well-supported by his wife, Marjorie, and together they had extended the hospitality of the Headmaster's house to Governors, staff, pupils and visitors alike, enabling them to mix freely and to share their different perspectives of the school. He had confirmed the school's reputation as an educational, a cultural and a caring community, one in which staff and pupils alike could develop and flourish – the latter whilst preparing for the wider world of adulthood and work.

When Keith retired at the end of the Summer Term 1996, the school saw the departure of a distinguished generation of teachers: Keith himself, David Davies (1959), Antony Clark (1960), Alan Taylor (1961) and David Griffiths (1969). Ken Jerred, for 25 years the much-respected school porter, and his wife Ruth, both good friends to many teachers and boys, also took their well-earned retirement. The 1960s and 1970s were finally over at Haberdashers'. Another link with the past was broken in 1997 with the death of the Anonymous Donor. Only then did the school learn his identity. R.W. Diggens OBE was an OH Grenadier Guardsman who in 1940 had demolished bridges to delay the Nazi advance through France and had been one of the last British soldiers evacuated from Dunkirk. During his supremely successful post-war career in business he had delighted to describe himself as 'a tough cookie'.

Keith's successor was Jeremy Goulding. He was well prepared for the post. Born in 1950, educated in classics at the Beckett School, Nottingham, he read philosophy and theology at Oxford, where he was Captain of Boats at Magdalen in a year when the college contained several rowing 'Blues', and in 1974 began his teaching career at Abingdon School. In 1978 he moved to Shrewsbury School, where he became Head of Divinity and a boarding-house master, and in 1989 was appointed Headmaster of Prior Park College, Bath. The first lay head of that famous and highly successful Roman Catholic school, he had further improved its reputation, raised its pupil numbers, and guided it through the aftermath of what could have been a disastrous fire.

Jeremy Goulding, Headmaster, 1996–2001

He had emerged triumphant from three interviews with the Governors, but unlike Keith he knew little of Haberdashers' and no one in the school knew him. Aware of people's possible apprehension, between his appointment as Headmaster in 1995 and arrival at Haberdashers' in September 1996 he followed Keith's example of visiting the school many times, familiarising himself with its personalities and policies, and allowing its teachers and some of its senior pupils to get to know him.

At the end of his first year, he gave *Skylark* his impressions of Haberdashers'; its 'sheer size', its 'speed and space', its 'powerful sense of community' and its 'sense of friendliness and generosity'. He declared 'My aim is to sustain this as a thriving school, balancing the academic results, which are so important, with the vast array of activities and opportunities available here.' In addition to his own experience and position, he had two other

Geography Field Trip.

important points of perspective, for his wife Isobel taught in the school (the first Head's wife to do so) and one of his sons was a pupil in the school (the first Head's son since Tom's time).

Little by little he built up his team, from September 1996 working with the new Bursar, Malcolm Gilbertson, and from September 1998 with Simon Boyes as Second Master and Jon Corrall as Senior Master. But however much he relied on their ability to provide him with detailed advice and information, he knew that it was his role to take the lead, to solve immediate problems and to seize fleeting opportunities, besides being the school's principal ambassador, manager and long-term strategist. That role involved hard work and long hours, a burden that he shouldered conscientiously.

Early in 1996 Keith had produced a Development Plan, in part intended to explore the problems likely to be caused by the possible end of the Assisted Places Scheme. When the Labour government elected in 1997 abolished the APS in 1998 the Governors immediately replaced it with a system of bursaries linked to boys' academic potential and families' financial circumstances. In 1997 Jeremy initiated a Pastoral Review and the Governors approved a five year Building Development Plan to expand the Preparatory School (achieved by Easter 2001) and to replace the 1961 Science Block and the 1971 Technology Block. In 1999 he began to prepare his own Development Plan and to enlist staff support for its implementation. Seventy-three members of staff, operating in 12 working groups, gathered evidence and took soundings on most aspects of the school's curricular and extra-curricular life and, after engaging in unfettered debate and discussion, reported in June 2000.

Their work coincided with the first full-scale inspection since the early 1960s, for a week in October 1999. Jeremy's preparation was meticulous, calming the nervous, drawing on his own experience as an HMC Inspector, and explaining that he hoped for 'business as usual' during inspection week. The Lead Inspector, Brian P. Fitzgerald, was both a former pupil and a former teacher at the school, so was obliged to retain his authority and credibility by being entirely neutral and objective. The Inspection Report concluded: 'This is a very good school with many strengths and the Headmaster is vigorous and enthusiastic and leads in a refreshingly purposeful style.'

Pastoral Review, Development Plan and Inspection Report each helped to clarify Jeremy's ideas and policies. He believed that 'we must offer the best possible school curriculum and foster a sense of community'. To improve upon an already excellent state of affairs would not be easy. The Middle School curriculum used an option system to allow some specialisation in accordance with boys' abilities, interests and career plans, yet to give them a broad and balanced education for as many years as practicable. Sixth form general studies, offering courses as diverse as cookery and car maintenance, provided a complement to examination work. The school's ever-widening geographical catchment area and its ethnic and religious diversity had proved compatible with a sense of school community as boys accepted the equality and legitimacy of other cultures and traditions.

In August 1996 Haberdashers' had topped the Advanced Level league table published in The Times. This put the school in a doubtless deserved and certainly welcome but rather exposed position, so provoked discussion about the nature of the school's academic standard

A School and Community Service visit.

Charity chess.

and success. Since the mid-1980s the school had experienced an increase in the percentage of pupils being awarded 'A' and 'B' grades at GCSE and Advanced Level, yet the number of boys being admitted to Oxford and Cambridge had remained roughly stable.

Some teachers ascribed this dichotomy to better services provided by examination boards (syllabuses, mark schemes, examiners' reports and feedback meetings for teachers had improved beyond recognition), and to the two ancient universities' continued skill in assessing ability and potential. Others argued that GCSE work had become easier, emphasising technique rather than content, obliging Haberdashers' to modify its Socratic approach to Advanced Level teaching, and to adopt a more didactic style. Jeremy gave his full support to teachers, monitoring pupil progress and requesting parental cooperation in academic and in behavioural matters.

To some extent the government took responsibility for the sixth form curriculum out of Jeremy's hands by introducing the AS plus A2 system at 16+, according to which AS is a transition from GCSE to Advanced Level standard at A2. Since September 2000 most Haberdashers' sixth formers have taken four AS courses in the Lower Sixth and from September 2001 three A2 courses in the Upper Sixth. That has proved a welcome simplification of the previous system in which the different examination boards had set their examinations virtually throughout the year without coordination.

The 1997 Pastoral Review and the Inspection Report led to further improvements to the system of pastoral care. From September 2001 the composition of third, fourth and fifth form tutor groups was no longer determined by academic setting, in an all-too obvious hierarchy of academic esteem, but was linked directly to the Houses, facilitating closer cooperation between Tutors and Housemasters, and the Tutors were given the opportunity to take a fuller part in giving advice on career planning, subject choice and work experience, so bringing them into even closer contact with pupils and parents, a desirable situation for all concerned.

Throughout these changes and improvements, the school's everyday activities had continued. As *Skylark* put it in 1997, 'life continues in a certain timeless fashion around us' – art, drama, music and sport, CCF, exchanges, mountaineering and ski-trips, carol service, Mencap Funday, Senior Citizens' Christmas Party and Staff Charity Concert, assemblies, Houses and societies, and staff arrival and departures. Pam Bryant, Michael Levin and Michael McLoughlin retired in 1997, John Carleton and Derrick Swann in 1998, and Douglas Whittaker and Stephen Wilkins in 2000; every one of them after more than 20 years' service at the school, with John and Douglas after a memorable 38 and 36 years respectively.

In July 2001 Jeremy left too, after having been invited to return to Shrewsbury as Headmaster. Although he had served Haberdashers' for only five years, he had made his mark. A family man, he knew the difficulties that pupils and parents can cause for teachers. When dealing with problems of all types he valued the facts, sought the truth, and strove for just solutions. He did not take the easy option. That the pupils who knew

The cast of *Company*, Senior School play 1998.

ABOVE: Preparatory School artists. INSET: Prep art lesson in the School grounds.

CLOCKWISE FROM TOP: Practical design; cricket; information technology lesson.

ABOVE: Athletics. INSET: Junior hockey team at the annual summer workshop.

Drama at Haberdashers'. CLOCKWISE FROM TOP LEFT: On stage; behind the scenes; Junior School play, *A Midsummer Night's Dream*.

FACING PAGE: First World War Memorial in Aldenham House.

SERVE AND OBEY

TO THE GLORIOUS MEMORY OF THE BOYS OF
THIS SCHOOL WHO OBEYED THE CALL OF FREE
DOM AND HONOUR AND SERVED UNTO DEATH

ADAMS, J.W	DAKERS, J	LAWRIE, N.E	ROSS, N.L
AVERY, W.E	DAVIES, R.W	LEHMAN, R.R	ROSS, R
AWBERY, C.L	DEFRECE, C	LEVY, C	RUSSELL, W.D
BALDWIN, W.E	DEW, A.W	MANN, F.C	SANDERSON, F.W
BARDER, S.G	DEWDNEY, H	MAXWELL, J	SELBY, M.G
BARRETT, J.H.P	ELLERTON, B.H	McARTHUR, D	SHARP, A.C
BAUMGARTNER, A.W	ELLERTON, F.G	McILVRIDE, N.J	SPEAR, N.V
BENSCHER, G.A	EMES, D.W	MICHELSEN, A.C	SUTTON, D.J.R
BIRCH, C.L	ESPURY, A	MIEVILLE, G.F	SWIFT, T.E
BOND, S.G	FLOREY, Q.M	MILNE, F.J	TAYLOR, L.F
BRAND, H	GILLESPIE, L.H.G	MOGFORD, L.W	TOFIELD, C.A
BRETTON, H.G	GRANT, E.H	MORRIS, A.J	TOOP, R. W
BROWN, L.V	GREEN, M	MORRIS, R.M	VALLANCEY, R.V
BURT, C.V	GREIFFENHAGEN, N	MOSES, F.S	VARNDELL, L.I
CARTER, E.R	GUNN, J.H	MOSS, H.W	VICK, K.J
CARTER, W.J.S	HAGGIS, C.G	PATEY, H.A	VINE, E.S.L
CHAMBERLAIN, J.H	HARTLEY, N.T	PATEY, S.E	VINEY, R.A
CHAPPELL, L.W	HEILBRON, V.J	PATTERSON, A	WHITE, F.W
CHURCHOUSE, P	HEMINGWAY, E.W	POWELL, R.W	WALTON, F.J.G
CLINCH, H.E	HILL, W.V	PURVER, F.J	WALTON, R.F
COULES, E.A.G	HODSON, F.G	RAMUS, E.I	WATERSON, E
CRAWLEY, A	HUMPHREYS, V.R	REID, W.M	WYATT, C
CUTMORE, W.C	HASLOP, T	RETALLACK-MOLONEY, H.R	YOUNG, H.M
DAKERS, E	JOSEPH, W.G.A	RIGHTON, R.H	YOUNG, V.H

ARTAUD, G.F.D
HUDSON, F.J.D
KIRTON, W.H
LETTY, R
MORISON, A.J
BARKER, H.F

1914   1918

Combined Cadet Force on an assault course.

CLOCKWISE FROM TOP: Science experiment; the end of a long school day; chess tournament.

Cricket in front of Aldenham House.

A scene from the Junior School play, *The Rebels of Gas Street*, 1999.

him best appreciated his efforts was apparent from his enthusiastic welcome to the Prefects' Dinner held in June 2001 and from the generous presentation made to him. The teachers appreciated his attention to detail, his diligent hard work, his diplomacy and his vision for the school – care, curriculum and community. Many of us will remember Jeremy at the Spring Term Concert in 2001: a man at ease with himself, playing the cello, supported by his wife and younger son as fellow musicians, supporting the school's rich extra-curricular life, making his customary apposite and fluent speech, and then helping to entertain the throng with his typical mixture of gentlemanly courtesy, good humour and tact. Haberdashers' loss was Shrewsbury's gain.

It was a fitting tribute to his service and stewardship that shortly after the examination results were published in August 2001 The Sunday Times chose Haberdashers' as its 'School of the Year' and produced a recognisable description.

It had an outstanding year in public examinations. Of all GCSE entries, 85.6% returned A* or A grades, an astonishing 50% at A*. Advanced level performance was also impressive: 89.8% A and B grades, 72% A's. The recent inspection highlighted the school's 'happy and purposeful atmosphere' and its 'sense of community'. Inspectors found teachers shared a 'warm and friendly rapport' with the pupils. It has a broad cultural and ethnic mix from a 15-mile radius. It has a 100-acre site with extensive woodlands. The neighbouring Haberdashers' Aske's School for Girls is close enough for cooperation across a range of activities.

13

Haberdashers' Today

2001–

After Jeremy left in July 2001, Simon Boyes ably and calmly served as acting Headmaster until Peter Hamilton arrived at the start of the Summer Term 2002. Educated at King Edward VI School, Southampton, and Christ Church, Oxford, he had taught modern languages at Radley College and Westminster School, before returning to King Edward's as Headmaster, from where he moved to Haberdashers'.

It has fallen to Peter to act on the findings of the 1999 inspection, by further improving the school's pastoral system, and to host the 2005 inspection, which acknowledged his achievement, and from which Haberdashers' naturally emerged unscathed, besides introducing his own development plans, which encourage the use of ICT as an aid to effective academic work. He has overseen the construction of the magnificent Aske Building, opened by Lord Brittan in May 2004, which contains 'state of the art' geography, ICT and science classrooms, laboratories and workshops, not to mention a new Staff Common Room, and which has contributed much to an already excellent environment for teaching and learning.

A notable feature of recent years has been the further development of the Preparatory School. Basil Flashman's successors (Mark Catley, Pam Bryant and Yvonne Mercer) have cultivated cricket and soccer, drama and music, and activities of all kinds play a key part in the Prep. boys' education. During the 2005 Easter Holiday 16 boys took part in a memorable cricket tour to Barbados. In 2006 Tom Senior won the British under-10 British Chess Championship. The Prep.'s exceptional curricular and extra-curricular quality was recognised in November

Morning in the Coach Park.

2006 when *The Sunday Times* awarded it the accolade of 'Preparatory School of the Year', in effect confirming the Governors' recent decision to open a Pre-Prep. School, congratulating Yvonne Mercer and her staff, and complementing the main school's own award.

Meanwhile, the main school's daily life continues in 2007 much as it did in 1997. Academic excellence has pride of place: Haberdashers' A* and 'A' grade rating at GCSE generally approaches 90%, 'A' grade rating at Advanced level is normally nearly 80%, and about 40 boys a year usually enter Oxbridge, but the School recognises the truth of the well-known proverb that 'All work and no play makes Jack a dull boy.' Indeed, part of Haberdashers' quality, and its popularity with boys and parents, is its range and richness of sports and other activities, from which the whole school community benefits enormously.

Rugby and cricket long benefited from the dedication of Douglas Yeabsley (Captain of England Schools' Cricket 1960, member of Devon CCC 1959–89). During December and January 1981/82 he led the first of many Haberdashers' sports tours to the Far East. Described by Ian Botham as 'the second-best left-arm bowler in England', in June 2000 he received the unusual honour of a personal profile in the sports pages of *The Times*. From 1989 to 1996 Clive Rees (British Lions, Wales, Barbarians, London Welsh and Berkshire) coached the 1st XV with panache and style all of his own. Ali Metcalfe, a Cambridge Blue, now coaches the 1st XV.

Hugh Pearman played cricket for St Andrews, was awarded a Blue whilst at Cambridge, played for the Oxford and Cambridge XI against the West Indian tourists, and from 1964 to 1972 turned out on occasion for Middlesex CCC. At Haberdashers' Keith Talbot persuaded him to help with hockey and he coached many teams to success, benefiting from a second AstroTurf pitch. Cricket has lately reflected Stephen Charlwood's careful organisation, Michael Yeabsley's coaching and many boys' devotion to the game. At the end of the 2006 season the 1st XI was one of only three unbeaten school sides in Britain and The

Peter Hamilton, Headmaster 2002– .

BELOW LEFT: Art in the School grounds.

RIGHT: Lower School science.

Times placed it second in quality only to Harrow School, long known for its superb cricket.

Trevor Hyde, who in 2001 won the National Council for School Sport's Sports Teacher of the Year award, has led water polo to national success. At the end of the 1996/97 season Haberdashers' U-19 team won the English Schools championship. Not surprisingly, Matthew Irish captained the England Junior Water Polo Team, and James Kattan the Great Britain Junior Team. During the 2001/02 season Tim Smith and John Beardsworth were selected for the England U-16 team. In 2005 the School U-19 team was runner-up in its age group in the English Schools championship, as was the U-15 team, a feat that it repeated in 2006.

Recently led by Andy Ward, association football has gone from strength to strength. In 2005 the 1st XI won the Crusader Cup by beating Rugby School 3-1, and celebrated with their most distant tour to date, three weeks in Brazil, including superb training, five tough matches, and some hectic social life. Under Steve Lowe's expert coaching, during 2006 athletics had its most successful season for years, and a strong U-16 team secured a magnificent second place in the final of the National English Schools Track and Field Cup competition.

Coached by Adrian Herzmark, badminton is also flourishing. In 2003 the U-14 team won the England Schools National Final at their age group and Kamran Huq was chosen to represent England at U-15 level. The next year he was joined by Nigel Tao, and the U-16 team won the English Schools National Final for their level, ably coached by Bob Welsh (President of Herts. Badminton) whilst Adrian was ill. Even more remarkably, the

Sport.

Chess coaching.

U-16s retained the championship in 2005. In both 2005 and 2006 Kamran and Nigel won a Bronze Medal for their performance in doubles at the U-17 National Championships.

The Bridge Club, coached by Paul Marx, triumphed during 2002/03: the 'A' team won the most prestigious trophy available to schools, the British Bridge League Schools Cup, and the 'B' team won the Schools Plate competition; not surprisingly, three players were selected for the England U-20 squad. The 'A' team retained the Cup in 2004 and 2005, but in 2006 narrowly lost in the final.

In 2003 the Chess Club unfortunately failed to retain the U-15 National Championship, and finished second. In 2004, however, it won the National Rapid Play U-14 and U-18 tournaments, and provided five members of various England teams. Chess was especially strong during 2006. Akash Jain emerged as the No. 1 U-12 player in Britain, Saravanam Sathyanandha was a member of the England U-12 team, and Vedantha Kumar, a sixth former, was a member of the England team that played in the historic city of Krakow, Poland.

During the year 2001/02 the Senior Debating Team of Nick Sloboda and Adam Berlin benefited from Jill Gleeson's expertise and won the Cambridge Union's Schools' Competition in which over 300 teams took part. This was followed by victory in the

Durham University Schools' Competition. Coincidentally, Jeremy Brier, a former team member, was elected President of the Cambridge Union, ably following Leon Brittan and Lance Foreman. In 2003 Jeremy won the World Debating Championships representing the Middle Temple, and in 2006 narrowly missed being chosen as the prospective Conservative Parliamentary Candidate for Watford, in succession to Ali Miraj, another OH, who had fought the seat in 2005 but in 2007 clashed with David Cameron, the party leader.

The same team also won the English Speaking Union's public-speaking competition for English schools, and then took first place in the International Final, beating Ireland, Scotland and Wales, so received the ESU's Silver Mace from the Duke of Edinburgh in Buckingham Palace, a fitting conclusion to an event involving over 500 schools. (Haberdashers' also won the Mace in 1977 and 1980, becoming the only school to have held it three times.)

James Fox (left) and Jamie Susskind (right).

In 2006 Jamie Susskind captained the English Schools' Debating team, and was judged the world's best speaker. During 2007 Haberdashers' debating and public speaking teams won a record number of competitions. Ben Lewy and James Fox won the Oxford Union Schools' Debating Competition, and Jamie Susskind and James Fox won the Cambridge and Durham Unions' Schools' Debating Competitions and the National Final of the

Cadets Assault Course at Elstree.

English Speaking Union's Public Speaking Competition – so Haberdashers' held the Mace for an unprecedented four times.

Each year teams chaperoned by Alex Simm take part in Model United Nations events at Haileybury College, Royal Russell School, St Andrew's School, Dublin, and The Hague, regularly winning best individual speaker and best delegation awards. In 2005 their oratorical skill contributed to the success of the school's Mock General Election. Guided by David Reid and Angela Bowen, a joint Boys' and Girls' School group attends the annual meetings of the European Youth Parliament, and in 2006 emerged as the best British team, so at Easter represented the UK in Paris. Advised by Kirti Shah, Haberdashers' team was runner-up in the national final of the Bank of England's '2.0' competition in both 2006 and 2007.

A great deal of time and energy is given to School and Community Service, not only in such obvious forms as the St John Ambulance Unit, in helping the disabled and visiting several care homes, but in charitable fund-raising events such as the Staff University Challenge and the Staff Charity Concert, six of which have been held since 1995 and usually raise over £2,000. The annual Senior Citizens' Christmas Party and Mencap Funday, which caters for children with learning disabilities, are run jointly with the Girls' School and attract scores of volunteer helpers.

A small but dedicated group goes on Duke of Edinburgh and Mountaineering Club expeditions, whereas the Combined Cadet Force has some 300 members. Its two hours of exercises and training on Friday afternoons represent only a small part of its role. More important are the three field days, each of which involves an overnight camp, the Easter adventure training in the hills at Otterburn in Northumbria, and the annual summer camp, in 2006 held in Yorkshire and in 2007 with the Fusiliers in Cyprus. The annual NCOs' dinner held in the Tower of London, and the CCF dinner, which is attended by many

Bourne Library, main reading room.

Old boys FROM LEFT: Adam Thirlwell, William Sutcliffe, David Baddiel, Matt Lucas.

OHs, held at the RAF Club in Piccadilly, are social highlights of the year. In November 2006 a group of OHs attended the Cadet Corps' Remembrance Day parade, laid a wreath at the Second World War Memorial, and joined the Officers and NCOs for tea in the Old Refectory, confirming a new tradition.

Each of the six Houses generates a multitude of events, as does each academic department, where exchanges, trips and visits are an integral part of each course. Drama and music, led by Tim Norton and Chris Muhley, are especially prolific. In 2006 *Macbeth*, the Senior School Play, *Beowulf*, the Middle School play, and *A Midsummer Night's Dream*, the Junior School play, were received with acclamation. As well as holding a multitude of regular concerts, our musicians arrange 'Lunchtime Live' each Friday, and hold an annual Music Festival to find the Haberdashers' Young Musician of the Year. Their special events are of the highest quality: during 2006 they held a Gala Concert at The Barbican and the Concert Band toured northern Italy. Much less formal events are the Unplugged Concert and Battle of the Bands, when the initiative passes to boys inspired by 'popular' music.

Maths holds regular conferences, physics an annual sixth form physics workshop and dinner, and in 2006 the Science Society had its most successful year ever, being addressed by numerous distinguished speakers. Captain Ben Aumonier OH spoke accompanied by a bomb disposal van, 'wheelbarrow' robot and protective suit, and described his work in army bomb disposal to a packed Aske Hall. Sixth form scientists write and edit *Scope*, our scientific and technical journal, and sixth form historians and economists write original articles for *Timeline* and *The Key*, whilst the English department has a creative writing magazine, *Scribe*.

A little-known aspect of Haberdashers' is the boy-author. In 2003 Laith Allawi published his illustrated novel *The Kingfisher and the Silver Dove*. In 2006 Toby Young won the Daunt Books short story competition with *The Skipping Rope*, and was awarded the BBC Proms—Guardian Young Composer of the Year award for his composition *Dirty Linoleum*, broadcast on Radio 3 in August. Will Gallimore, one of the school's promising all-round sportsmen, won the BBC's Young Sports Journalist of the Year competition.

This literary enterprise links the school to successful Old Haberdashers'. In 1994 James Merino of New College, Oxford, was awarded the Newdigate Prize for Poetry, instituted in 1805 and won by some of the most famous British men of letters, including Oscar

Fun in the snow.

Wilde. William Sutcliffe's *New Boy* (1996), set its exploration of adolescent attitudes and values in a thinly disguised version of Haberdashers'. His next novel *Are You Experienced?* (1997) described his back-packing experiences and his third *The Love Hexagon* (2000) the social life of young professionals. When interviewed, he confessed to having been inspired to start reading seriously by studying *Macbeth* for O Level English Literature, but revealed an ambivalent relationship with the school: 'At first I hated it, but by the end I was happy there.'

He was not the first recent OH writer to be influenced by his years at Haberdashers'. John Gilmore, author of *Flying the Flag* (UK ed. 2003), recalls that he had mixed feelings about the Boarding House, but that his experience of the school as a whole was overwhelmingly positive. Oscar Moore's novel *A Matter of Life and Sex* (1992) attracted considerable attention for its literary quality, and for its realistic social commentary. In 2003 The Times anticipated the publication of Adam Thirlwell's first novel, *Politics*, by noting the contrast between his position as a Fellow of All Souls, Oxford, and the book's setting in north London suburbia, also Sutcliffe's chosen literary territory.

The school's best-known current literary genre is comedy. Matt Lucas has achieved fame with the award-winning cult programme *Little Britain*. Sacha Baron Cohen originally made his name as Ali G, but is now renowned for his role as Borat, the politically incorrect citizen of Kazakhstan. David Baddiel is known as a comedian, columnist, novelist and joint author of the unofficial England soccer song 'Three Lions', with its chorus of 'football's coming home'.

All these OHs except Lucas are Oxbridge graduates: Thirlwell, English (Oxford); Gilmore and Baron Cohen, history; Sutcliffe and Baddiel, English (Cambridge). Ashley Blaker, an OH history graduate of both Oxford and Cambridge, and a comedy scriptwriter, attributes their success to the interaction of two influences: on the one hand, able, dedicated and experienced teachers who give pupils the freedom to challenge and to discuss, and encourage verbal and written dexterity in lessons, debating and drama; on the other, the pupils' own emotional, intellectual and social confidence, secure in their sense of cultural and ethnic identity. Few other English schools have that combination or provide such an education.

The Governors intend to further improve the high quality of that education and to make it even more readily accessible. In 1991 the Haberdashers' Company obtained a further Scheme from the Charity Commissioners. The Company then formed the Haberdashers' Aske's Charity and the associated Hatcham Trust. It merged the Boys' and the Girls' schools at Hatcham into a City Technology College (1991) and converted it into an Academy (2005) at the same as creating the Haberdashers' Aske's Knights Academy at Downham. In 1998 an amendment to the 1991 Scheme clarified the arrangements for governing the Boys' and the Girls' schools at Elstree, creating a new common governing body and an executive committee for each school, introducing the innovative and valuable practice of including former pupils.

In 2006 the Boys' School set up the Haberdashers' Aske's Boys' School Foundation in order to raise funds to support the development of the school, and appointed a Director of External Relations. This coincided with plans to refine the school's admission procedures, to contact parents of potential pupils, to deepen links with existing parents and the OHs, and to consolidate the school's public profile both locally and nationally. The aim is to amass an endowment not only capable of providing for even more bursaries and scholarships than at present, but large enough to fund the school's future development programme, and so to avoid the shortage of money and periodic financial crises which have occasionally hindered the school during its long history.

The School's clock tower.

With about 1,300 pupils, Haberdashers' gives scholarships worth around £60,000, and grants some 200 bursaries worth nearly £800,000. The school would like to award more scholarships and bursaries, so more boys from families of modest means can benefit from the superb education that it provides and go on to make their own contribution to our national life, as have so many members of previous generations. Haberdashers' would also like to replace the remaining early 1960s buildings to complement the superb educational facilities provided by the Music School, the Preparatory School, the Bourne Building and the Aske Building. Taken together, these policies will preserve the best of the school's ethos and heritage, fitting both to the needs of the twenty-first century.

It is instructive to revisit three elements in Haberdashers' history. In 1689 Robert Aske's Will provided for '20 poore Boyes'. The 1690 Act of Parliament laid down that they were to be taught 'Learning and good Manners'. In 1870 the Company acted on H.J. Roby's advice that a good school had an entrance exam open to all comers and 'exhibitions on a liberal scale so as to give the most promising boys an opportunity of rising into the rank for which their natural gifts fit them'.

Haberdashers' has remained faithful to those three elements. The school supports boys who would not otherwise be able to afford the education it provides for them. Its first class education introduces boys to academic excellence and all-round personal development. It allows them to achieve their full potential.

In the words of the school prospectus quoted by the Headmaster, our aim is 'To challenge bright boys to achieve the highest standards, to develop a sense of community and shared values, and to support parents in preparing their sons for a fulfilled life.' That aim provides Haberdashers' vision for the future.

List of Subscribers

E.J.T. ACASTER
ANISH ACHARYA
D. ACKERMAN
HAMISH ADAM
DR ROBERT ADAMS
WILLIAM ALDRED
TONY ALEXANDER
P. ALTERMAN
NIKHIL AND SANEEL AMIN
LANCE ANISFELD
MATTHEW ANISFELD
OLIVER ANISFELD
W.E. (BILL) APTED
CLIVE H. ASTON
PAUL AND ROMAINE ASTRUC
RICHARD H. AUTERAC
A. BEARE
JAMES BEATTIE
CLIVE BENDER
MICHAEL BEN-GERSHON
      (FORMERLY COHEN)
R.A. BENSON
RUPERT BERRYMAN
CHARLIE BETTERIDGE
A.S. BHOHI
M. BIBER
BARRY BINGHAM
LYNN BIRD
C.M. BISHOP
JOHN BLACKBURN
GARY BLAKER
P.P. BLAND
ANDREW BLESSLEY
SIMON BOYES
D.H. BRAHMBHATT
IAN BRENT
JACK BRESLAUER
R.C.P. BROOKHOUSE
STUART C. BROWN
MALCOLM BROWN
N.J. BROWN
NIGEL C. BROWN
PAMELA BRYANT
S. BUTCHER
JAMES BUTLER
RUSS CANNING
PETER CAREY
T.F.A. CARTER MCMI
ROBERT H.S. CATTLE
AJANTHA CHANDRASENA

J.T. CHARALAMBOUS
J.A. CHARLES
KEITH G. CHEYNEY
MICHAEL CLARK
SIMON CLARKE
MICHAEL CLEVELAND
JOHN W. COGGINS
RICHARD COHEN
JON, DAN AND BEN COLMAN
JONATHAN CONSTANTINOU
PETER COOK
DENNIS COOPER-JONES
JON CORRALL
JAMES COSTI
ANDREW COX
K.C. CURTIS
ROBERT J. DABOUL
JOHN DAVENEY
DAVID DAVIDSON
K.G. DAVIES
J.M. DAVIS
BARRY J. DAVISON
KEITH DAWSON
MICHAEL DAY
MIKE DAY
TOM DEAN
RAVI DESAI
DR ARTHUR DEWAR
JORDAN DIAS
MIKE DICHLIAN
H.R. DOBBS
NERAL DODHIA
JAMES M. DONAGHEY
ALAN DORMAN
BIKARAM S. DOSANJH
S. DUA
MARTIN DUNITZ
MAURICE DWEK
BRUCE EADIE
DAVID EAGAR
PAUL J. EAGAR
PAUL EAGLES
SIMON EAGLES
BERNARD EDER
RICHARD EDWARDS
HENRY EDWARDS
P.J. EGAN
ANDREW ELLINAS
T.A.A. ELLIOTT
PAUL ELSTER

ANDREW EVANS
JOHN H. EVANS
MARTIN C FAIRLEY
ANDREW FALCONER
JOHN FELTHAM
JAMES FENNER
ARTHUR FIBER
BEN JACK FINGER
B.J. FLETCHER
VERNON FLYNN
JOHN N. FODEN
PAUL FOSTER
ALAN FOX
PETER H. FRANK
JOHN FRANKLIN
PHILIP FREEBORN
CHARLES FREEMAN
JOHN E. FREEMAN
PETER FREITAG
NICK FRENCH
SIMON GARFIELD
ANNE GARSIDE
DESMOND GASKELL
J.B. GASKELL
JULIAN GLICHER
DR ANN VICTORIA GODDARD
NICHOLAS GODMAN
RORY GOFF
CHONG GOH
CHRISTINA GOLDIE
P.G.B. GRANT
GIANCARLO GRASSO
MICHAEL GRENFELL
D.J. GRIFFITH
DAVID GRIFFITHS
ANUND GUDKA
RAVI GUPTA
CRAIG HALL
NIGEL HALL
GEORGE HALLER
PETER HAMILTON
J.J. HANSON
MR SANDIP HARIA
CHRISTOPHER HARRIS
JONATHAN DAVID HARRIS CBE
ROBERT J. HARRIS
BENEDICT HARRISON
DAVID B. HASSELL
JEREMY HAVARDI
JOHN S. HAWKES

GERRY HEGAN
MICHAEL HEPPNER
JAMES HERRING
JOHN HITCHIN
PHILIP G. HOARE
DANIEL HOCHBERG
ADRIAN L.A. HOGAN
SIMON HOLLINS
NICK HOLMES
RON HORNE
SAM HUSSAIN
SIMON HYDE
TREVOR HYDE
LUCA IGNATIUS
MARC C. ISAACS
M.G.A. JACK
RODNEY B. JAKEMAN
E.A. JAMES
NORMAN A.H. JAMES
JUN LOK WONG JASPER
EDWARD JEANS
M.H.V. JEANS
JEREMY JEEVES
CHRISTOPHER G. JENKINS
DUNCAN JENKINS
MAX JENKINS
RICHARD JENKINS
GRAHAM B. JONES
K.P. JONES
NIKHIL DAVID JOSHI
JONATHAN KARMI
IMRAN KASSAM
PRASHANT KAUL
AIVAR KAULINS
MILES KAYE
ANDREW KEENLEYSIDE
BRYAN KEEP
STEPHEN R.D. KENNETT
F. JOHN KENT
ANTHONY KENWARD
SIMON KINDER
HARRY KINGDON
JOHN KINGSTON
RICH AND SUSAN KINGDON
ALASDAIR KIRK
DANIEL KIRK
REV JOHN KIRKBY
DAVID KITCHEN
LAWRENCE KLEMPA
NAZ KLENDJIAN

CANON JOHN KNOWLES-BROWN
ANTHONY KO
STEPHEN KO
D.P. KORN
ALEXANDER KUPFER
WILLIAM KUPFER
DEMETRIOS KYRIACOU
MARIOS KYRIACOU
SIR DENNIS LANDAU
R.N. LANYI
FRED LAST
KEITH LAW
MR AND MRS J. LAWRENCE
R.M. LAWSON
DR IAN C. LEIGH
MELVIN LOUIS AND JEREMY LEONG
KEITH LEVERTON
BEN, GUY AND JACK LEWY
ROY LIDINGTON
ERNEST L. LITTAUER
KEN LOWE
IAN D. LUDER
MARSHALL LUMSDEN
ROGER LYLE
HEMANG MAJEETHIA
N.K. MALDE
RICHARD MARTIN
OLIVER M. MARTIN
JOZSEF MARTON
NICHOLAS PAUL MASON
JOHN A. MATHEWS
ROBIN MATTHEW
MICHAEL G. MAX
DR JOHN MCELWAINE FRCA
HAMISH MCGECHAN
MR RYAN MCINTOSH
HUSEIN AND ZAYN MEGHJI
DILESH B. MEHTA
CLIFTON MELVIN
PETER W. MITCHELL
M.J. MILNER
STUART M.C. MOORE
EDWARD MOORES
DAVID MORGAN
PATRICK MORIARTY
JOHN LEWIS MORLEY
MICHAEL MORRISH
EDWARD MORRISON

J.B. MULCHRONE
DR H. MULLINS
PAUL B. MURPHY
ROHAN M. MURPHY
JAMIE MURRAY
ADAM NASH
OLIVER NASH
RUJU NATHWANI
SINGHAL NEER
A.G. NEWMAN
DAVID NICHOLLS
GREG NUNAN
JOHN W. NUTTALL
RONALD NYE
KEITH ALAN ODY
DR NICHOLAS PALUCH
NIRAL CHANDU PANCHAL
NICHOLAS PARKER
N. ROGER PARKER
ASHISH PARMAR
NITIN PARMAR
PHILLIP PARR
KRISTIAN PARRY
FRANK M. PARTINGTON
RONALD E. PARTINGTON
FAADIL PATEL
MITUL PATEL
NEIL PATTERSON
A.V. PEACOCK
LEE PETERSON
G. PETKEN
MR G. PICKERING
SIMON PINNER
IAN POWELL
DOMINIC PRESTON
HENRY PRESTON
GORDON RAISIN
PROFESSOR F.H. READ
SAMUEL N. REISMAN
IAN MOGER RICKWOOD
DR DAVID RIDGE
D.H. RIDGEON
LT. COL. N.J. RIDOUT
DEBORAH RIVLIN
DIANA ROBERTSON
JOHN A. ROBBINS
JANE ROBSON
THOMAS J. ROBSON
A.I. RODGERS
DAVID ROSEN

NICHOLAS ROYCE
ANTHONY RUMFORD
OLIVER RUSSELL
MICHAEL C. RYAN
PAUL SALTER
ROBERT SAMUELSON
JAMES SANT
ARISTO SAVVA
NICHOLAS RICHARD SCARLES
RONALD SCARLES
MARGARET SCRIBBINS
MALCOLM SETTON
DR K. SHAH
KUSHAL SHAH
PARAS SHAH
RIKIN D. SHAH
SAHIL D. SHAH
SAJAN SHAH
SHAJEEN SHAILENDRA
G. SHAW
SALMAN SHEIKH
ANTHONY D. SHERIDAN
ALEX SHERR
MATTHEW SHERR
HITEN GYANDEV SHETH
SUNIL SHETH
A.D. SILVERBECK
ROGER F. SKINNER
IAN SMART
ROGER SMITH
ARJUN SOFAT
PETER SPENCE
ROBERT SPOKOINI
G. (HENRY) STEINHARDT
PETER J. STEVENSON
LEWIS STOCK
MARK STOCKER
PHILIP STOCKS
DR CAROLE STOREY
SIVANANTHAN SUBON
J.W. SUCKLING
ROYALTON SUMMERFIELD
JAMES SWAFFIELD
JOHN SWALLOW
JEREMY SWINNERTON TAYLOR
ANDREW G. TAIT
RONEL TALKER
D.M. TAMMAN
NEIL RAVI TANNA

REX TASKER
LAURENCE R. THACKRAY
NIKHIL THADANI-SIX
KEITH THOMPSON
G.C. THOMPSON
GRAHAM THOMPSON
C.K. THONG
PROF B.A. THRUSH
JOHN TITFORD
SEAN TOMLIN
RICHARD TOOMER
TIM TSUNG
MICHAEL TYLER
CHARLIE UGO
JORDAN URBAN
EFOSA UWAIFO
JOHN W. VALENTINE
DR MALCOLM VANDENBURG
JOHN VINCENT
ANDREW P.D. WALKER
ROGER WALTERS
HARRY WALTON
M.R. WARMAN
E.J. WARREN
OLIVER WARREN
D.W. WELLS
DAVID WESTCOUGH
M.J. WESTON
J.G. WHITEHEAD
G.T. WICKENS
LAURENCE WICKS
B.E. WILSON
SHAUN WILSON
ALEX R. WOOD
HEATHER WOOD
A.A.G. WOODFORD
JEROME WOODWARK
MARTYN M. WOOLF
ALAN WOOLFORD
MATTHEW WORBY
PETER WRIGHTON
PETER WULFF
PETER A.H. WYATT
STEVEN YANKELSON
D.I. YEABSLEY
M.I. YEABSLEY
R.S. YEABSLEY
MARTIN ZUCKER

Index

Entries for illustrations are denoted in *italics*